Birds of
Kenya's Rift Valley

Adam Scott Kennedy

PRINCETON

press.princeton.edu

Published by Princeton University Press,
41 William Street, Princeton, New Jersey 08540
In the United Kingdom: Princeton University Press, 6 Oxford Street,
Woodstock, Oxfordshire OX20 1TW
nathist.press.princeton.edu

British Library Cataloging-in-Publication Data is available

Library of Congress Control Number 2013950247
ISBN 978-0-691-15907-2

Production and design by **WILD**Guides Ltd., Old Basing, Hampshire UK.
Printed in Singapore

10 9 8 7 6 5 4 3 2 1

For my birding friends in the Rift Valley,
Steve & Vicky Rose, Karen & Patrick Plumbe
and the amazing Francis Cherutich at Lake
Baringo. Happy Birding folks!

Contents

BIRDS OF WOODLAND, SCRUB AND GARDEN (continued)

African Fish Eagle

Squacco Heron

About this book

Twenty-six years before these words were written, a bird-mad schoolboy in England was completely mesmerised by a BBC TV series about Africa's Great Rift Valley that explored the wildlife of the lakes and wilderness of the region. I remember the Hippos, the Northern Red Bishops and the African Fish Eagles from that series so clearly and I remember vowing to myself that one day I would see it all for real. In April 2010 I finally did.

The birdlife of the Rift Valley is simply AMAZING! It never fails to impress me on every visit, and I am not alone with that sentiment. The pioneering American ornithologist Roger Tory Peterson described the sight of over a million flamingos at Lake Nakuru as "the greatest bird spectacle on earth" and for those thousands of people who have been fortunate enough to witness the spectacle, they will remember it forever too, such is the awe of an experience that can only be enjoyed in Kenya's Rift Valley.

Being the type of birdwatcher who likes to record as many species as possible (some call me a twitcher but I'm just a fanatical birder in my opinion!), it was not just the sight of the flamingos that won my heart. Some major rarities live in the Rift Valley, such as the Grey-crested Helmetshrike and Sharpe's Longclaw, but I recall being equally excited about finding my own Little Rock Thrush in Nakuru, Verreaux's Eagle at Baringo and Black-necked Weavers at Magadi for the very first time. The whole area is full of very beautiful birds and there is always a lot to find and observe. Even on a quiet day, the majesty of the lakes, volcanoes, waterfalls and cliffs of this geologically active region will entertain and delight.

After many visits to the various Rift Valley lakes, I always look forward to returning to my favourite, Lake Baringo, to catch up with friends and familiar faces, as well as world-class birding. My first visit to Baringo was a real birding success because of one person, my guide Francis Cherutich. A sizeable group of young bird guides now work in the Kampi ya Samaki area of Baringo and although I will always go birding with Francis (if he's not already booked up) I hear that most guides leave a lasting good impression on their guests. You cannot beat local knowledge in a place like Baringo as the guides know where, when and how to find the many species on their local patch and I cannot recommend the practice of using a local guide highly enough. Not only is it beneficial for you and the guide, it is great for the local economy and ensuring that communities place a high value on the bird life in their area. I have listed some local guides at various sites in the Rift at the rear of this book. My apologies to those guides who are not included in this edition but space does not permit this list being more comprehensive.

Some purists may grumble about the exclusion of Lakes Turkana and Natron in this guide so here is a quick explanation as to the reason why. Lake Turkana is so far from the main tourist areas elsewhere in the Rift Valley that very few tourists and birders head that way. Lake Natron does poke its northern shore over the Kenyan national border but over 99% of that lake is in Tanzania and special arrangements are needed to access the area from Kenya.

This guide is intended to be an inspirational, portable and easy-to-use introduction to the many hundreds of species that have been recorded in the Rift Valley. It is not intended to be comprehensive and the many species I have chosen to omit are either scarce or simply difficult to find and identify for the novice, such as many of the 'little brown jobs' (or LBJs).

In this book I have tried my level best to avoid OTJ – 'ornithological techno-jargon'. My wife Vicki was not a birder when I met her and, in polite company at least, will not confess to being one now. But her interest in birds has grown and she is now quite capable of identifying most of the species illustrated in this book. However, the minute I start pointing out greyish *supercilia*, spotted *median coverts* and ochre *rectrices* (all classic OTJ), she switches off. I firmly believe that it doesn't help to bore people about birds when they're starting out. By all means share the really interesting stuff and your own personal experiences but leave the OTJ for those who understand the language you're talking about. Serious birders may sneer at some of the simple terms I have used, but if Vicki and the uninitiated can understand them, anyone can – and that is what this book is all about. For this reason, I have opted not to include a diagram of the feathers and body parts of a bird (definitely OTJ) as I hope that everyone using this book will know the difference between a head, a wing and a tail.

As you can probably tell by now, I have tried to keep this book as light-hearted as possible and there are several pieces of text that I hope will raise a smile. After all, the life of birds and the people who named them are fascinating and, believe it or not, quite entertaining too! Ultimately, my hope is that you will get out there and enjoy the birdlife of Kenya's Rift Valley as much as I do. Happy Birding!

About the images

In collating the photos for this book, I have tried to capture and include the most suitable images to show the variations in sex, age and plumage throughout the year (for example, breeding and non-breeding plumages), both within and between the species. Where I have failed to capture the bird in a desired plumage or pose, the lovely people at **WILD**Guides have very kindly liaised with Greg & Yvonne Dean and Andy & Gill Swash at WorldWildlifeImages.com and obtained the images required. For that I am very grateful to all concerned, as these photos complement the book beautifully. Thanks also to Vicki for letting me use some of her images, which are wonderful. All the images that were not taken by me are fully credited on *page 246*.

Lesser Flamingos taking off
at Lake Bogoria.

How to use this book

Introducing well over 300 species of birds in an easy-to-use format comes with a few important presentation decisions but none more so than the order in which to place them within the book. Accordingly, the Princeton **WILD**Guides team and I agreed to continue the habitat-based approach that I adopted for my first field guide, *Birds of the Masai Mara*, which is a very practical approach that assumes no prior knowledge of the order followed in most field guides, the systematic list. One of the problems associated with a habitat-based approach is that birds are inherently mobile and frequently move around from one habitat to another. For this reason, the highly mobile swifts, swallows and martins have their own 'habitat' **Up in the air**, since that is where they spend the vast majority of their time, and the enigmatic **Birds of prey** also have their own special category because they frequently traverse numerous habitats in the course of a short flight. As collectives, these two bird groups are fairly straightforward to identify but others may be more problematic and this is where the habitat-based approach is most useful. **Night birds** also have their own section simply because they are most active when most other birds are not. This leaves us with three other main habitat sections; **Lakes and marsh, Grassland and open areas** and **Woodland, scrub and garden** that contain the bulk of the other species. The habitat sections in this book have been colour-coded in an attempt to make the process of finding your bird as simple as possible.

Understanding how the Rift Valley was formed, and the variety of habitats created as a result, really helps to understand why it is such a great place to watch birds. A short section on the geography of the region has therefore been included as well.

The English names used for the birds in this book are those adopted by the Bird Committee of Nature Kenya, as listed in the *Checklist of the Birds of Kenya (4th Edition)*. Since these may differ from the names given in other books, the most frequently used alternative English names are also given. Scientific names have not been included in the species accounts since they generally mean little to the average visitor. However, for those who are not familiar with English names but do know the scientific names, these names have been included in a list on pages *247–251*, cross-referenced to the relevant English name and page(s). The scientific names follow the *World Bird List* produced by the International Ornithologists' Union. The sizes shown for each bird indicate its length from the tip of the bill to the end of the tail and are given in both centimetres (cm) and inches ("). To help keep a record of the birds you see in the Rift Valley, a small tick-box has been included next to each species description.

Blue-cheeked Bee-eaters in typically alert mode.

Lake Elementeita – a
geography student's
dream, the scenery of the
Rift Valley rarely fails to
inspire and bewilder.

The geography of Kenya's Rift Valley

Hell's Gate

The Great Rift Valley is the name often given to the continuous trench that extends approximately 6,000 km (3,700 miles) from Syria in the north to Mozambique in the south. However, modern geologists will state that this is old thinking as the rift valley that extends southwards from Eritrea is quite separate from that which travels northwards through the Red Sea. Instead, we should be concentrating on the East African Rift that begins at the Afar Triangle (in Eritrea, Djibouti and Ethiopia) and finishes off the coast of Mozambique. This East African Rift is divided into two major branches: the western Albertine Rift, and the eastern Gregory Rift that is the Kenyan section often referred to as the Kenyan Rift Valley. This is the vast geological feature that runs north-south and splits Kenya in two, and the feature that is the emphasis of this guide.

The valley continues to be created by the divergence of two tectonic plates (*i.e.* vast pieces of the Earth's crust) caused by volcanic activity close to the Earth's surface. Not only has this volcanism created a number of deep and impressive valley features but also a number of imposing volcanoes in the region, including Mounts Kenya and Longonot in Kenya and Mount Kilimanjaro, Africa's highest mountain, in nearby Tanzania. This book focuses on the main valley system that extends from Lake Turkana in the north to Lake Magadi in the south, although other smaller, but still impressive, valleys do occur east and west, including the beautiful Kerio Valley that is also great for birding.

On either side of the deep valley are precipitous walls of rock, with the Elgeyo, Mau and Nguruman Escarpments to the west, and the Laikipia Escarpment, Aberdare Mountains and Ngong Hills to the east. Smaller cliff systems also abound and some, such as those in Hell's Gate National Park and those next to Lake Baringo, are great places for birding. The high ridges help to create a great deal of the rainfall that falls in the region and it is this water that collects in the heart of the Kenyan Rift Valley to create some of the most bird-rich lakes in Africa. These lakes are explored further on the following pages but it is important to explain here that because these water bodies are constrained within the valley walls they are not free-draining. This means that most lakes develop high concentrations of salts as the shallow waters evaporate.

Elevation also has an impact on the birdlife of the Rift Valley. With the peaks of various escarpments and mountains rising above 3,000 m / 9,800 ft above sea level (a.s.l.), they provide the right conditions for high-altitude species. Even areas at the bottom of the Rift Valley are at a surprising altitude, with the town of Naivasha standing at an impressive 1,890 m / 6,200 ft a.s.l., creating a relatively cool and temperate environment. This contrasts with the arid semi-desert environments found at the lowest areas of the valley, such as Lakes Baringo and Magadi that stand at altitudes of 1,000 m / 3,280 ft a.s.l. and 595 m / 1,952 ft a.s.l., respectively.

Lakes and marsh

It is probably fair to say that most birders and naturalists visiting the Rift Valley have a particular lake, or lakes, as the focus of any trip. Not only does each lake have its own unique geography but each has its own charisma and charm too. On every visit the local conditions, such as water level and the area of exposed mud, will differ, creating perfect conditions for some species and less suitable conditions for others. For this reason, the birds encountered may differ markedly between visits. As with any birding trip to East Africa, the time of year also has a big impact on the species you can expect to find. May to August are generally the quieter months in terms of the number of species that are likely to be seen, as this is when the northern migrants will be on their breeding grounds in Europe and Asia. October–November and February–March are the periods when many such migrants pass through the region and therefore the peak times for species counts. Lake water chemistry is vitally important for several species. This is particularly the case with flamingos which require soda lakes (*i.e.* those high in alkaline salts) and explains why they are generally absent from the freshwater Lakes Naivasha and Baringo. However, each lake has its own qualities that make it great for particular birds. The following descriptions of the major lakes, from north to south, contain generic area statistics. Whilst water levels vary considerably from year to year, the figures given are the maximum area when the lake is full.

Lake Baringo   altitude 1,000 m / 3,280 ft a.s.l.; area 170 km² / 66 sq. miles

This huge freshwater lake is among the most bird-rich of all the lakes featured here. There are extensive reedy margins that provide breeding habitat for a number of northern specials, such as **Northern Red Bishop** and **Northern Masked Weaver**, and a vast colony of herons and egrets in submerged trees at the southern end of the lake. A boat trip is highly recommended to access the heronry and the islands in the lake that hold **Senegal Thick-knee** and **Hemprich's Hornbill**, among others.

Lake Bogoria   altitude 990 m / 3,248 ft a.s.l.; area 34 km² / 13 sq. miles

This relatively small soda lake is popular for its geological features, such as geysers and hot springs, but it is the vast flocks of flamingos, often numbering in excess of 1 million birds, that are the major attraction here. **Pied Avocet** and **Cape Teal** are also often found in good numbers.

Lake Nakuru   altitude 1,760 m / 5,774 ft a.s.l.; area 50 km² / 19 sq. miles

Situated in the eponymous National Park, this soda lake is usually far less saline than both Bogoria and Magadi, making it attractive to species that favour soda and freshwater lakes. It has a healthy fish population that attracts vast flocks of **pelicans, cormorants** and **herons**, and sufficient algae and zooplankton to attract huge numbers of **flamingos** too. Numbers of **wildfowl**, **gulls** and **terns** vary through the year but can also be impressive. The combination of spectacular birdlife and big game make this one of the most popular places to visit in the Rift Valley.

Lake Elementeita   altitude 1,670 m / 5,479 ft a.s.l.; area 18 km² / 7 sq. miles

Situated between Nakuru and Naivasha towns, this shallow soda lake (sometimes called Elmenteita) is home to the most productive **Great White Pelican** colony in Kenya and often host to vast flocks of **flamingos**. Much of the lake's bird-rich shoreline, that holds many **wader** and **duck** species, lies within the Soysambu Conservancy. Spectacular views of the lake can be had from Sunbird Lodge, which also boasts fantastic birdlife in the gardens.

Lake Naivasha   altitude 1,890 m / 6,200 ft a.s.l.; area 155 km² / 60 sq. miles

This large freshwater lake has extensive woody and reedy margins that provide perfect conditions for **herons**, **kingfishers** and **gallinules**, among many others. The open water attracts various **duck** and **tern** species and many **waders** and grassland species occur along the lakeshore. This is a great place to get out on the water and there are many opportunities for boat trips here. Traditionally the most verdant of all Rift Valley lakes, Naivasha has suffered from excessive water extraction and pollution from the horticultural industry in recent years and unless these are kept in check, conservationists have warned that the lake may die off completely in the near future.

Lake Magadi   altitude 595 m / 1,952 ft a.s.l.; area 104 km² / 40 sq. miles

Set among some of the wildest semi-arid desert in southern Kenya, Magadi is the most alkaline of the Rift Valley lakes. The shoreline is encrusted with a thick white caustic salt and may give the impression that it is inhospitable for life. In fact, it is very rich in invertebrate life and host to many special birds including the scarce **Chestnut-banded Plover** that is difficult to find elsewhere in Kenya. It is readily accessible from Nairobi and a visit is highly recommended.

Stunning views and great birding reward the intrepid at Lake Magadi.

A flock of Little Swifts

Many birds can be seen flying from one place to another but there are two families of bird that spend most of their lives 'up in the air': the **swallows and martins** and the **swifts**. Because they can cover such large areas in the course of the day, these birds are likely to be encountered over many different habitats – but their true habitat is the sky where they feed and, in the case of swifts, even mate on the wing. Swallows and martins are also likely to be encountered close to lakes and marshes where flocks often gather to roost.

Birds of prey

Birds of prey, or raptors, are among many peoples'
favourite birds because they are often easy to spot
and many, especially vultures and eagles, evoke
a feeling of majesty and power. Like the species
covered in the *Up in the air* section, many spend a
great deal of time soaring and pass over a variety
of habitats as they do so. However, most have a
preferred environment in which to hunt.
For example, the **African Fish Eagle** requires
open areas of water and the small **(African)
Black-shouldered Kite** is a bird of open areas
and grassland. Identification of some species is
straightforward, while others, such as the **harriers**
and some **brown eagles**, can be more problematic.
To help you to make a positive identification,
in-flight photographs have therefore also been
included.

A Bateleur soars overhead, while a Rüppell's
Vulture surveys the scene.

Grassland and open areas

A multitude of grasses exist in the Rift Valley but from a very basic ecological perspective, it is useful to consider grasslands as either short or long, simply because birds either live and feed in long grass or on short grass.

Typically found at higher altitudes where higher rainfall and lower temperatures are conducive to growth, long grass provides plenty of cover in which birds can feed and nest, and also provides many with a nest-building medium. Many small birds abound, such as **cisticolas** and **Quailfinch**, and larger birds such as **storks** and **Southern Ground Hornbill** spend much of their time feeding in long grass. Another group of songbirds, the attractive **widowbirds**, thrive in the high-altitude grasslands in the Rift Valley and surrounding hills and escarpments.

Short grass generally means managed grass, especially when it is grazed by domestic livestock, such as cows and goats in the Maasai lands of the southern Rift. Elsewhere it may be grazed by wild game such as Zebra, Wildebeest and a variety of antelope. Birds living in such grazed environments are used to being exposed and are generally easier to observe, especially the **wheatears** and **chats**.

The term 'open areas' generally applies to those dry semi-arid places that are barely vegetated by grass and scrub but which are characterized by sand, stones and rocks, such as those in the Magadi and Baringo areas. They may appear inhospitable but actually provide perfect conditions for species such as **Heuglin's Courser** and **Pink-breasted Lark**.

Sharpe's Longclaw – a grassland specialist in steep decline

One of Kenya's most threatened birds has its last stronghold on the slopes of the Kenyan Rift and deserves a special mention here. The Sharpe's Longclaw is a Kenyan endemic (*i.e.* it is found nowhere else but Kenya) and was once common on the high-altitude tussock grasslands of the region. Numbers of the bird have fallen dramatically over the past 25 years as much of the suitable habitat has disappeared due to intensive grazing or cultivation to grow maize.

The ornithological team at Nature Kenya has been monitoring the species' decline and the most recent survey (2012) suggested that fewer than 500 birds remain. The final stronghold is the Kinangop Plateau, which is situated on the western slopes of the Aberdare Mountains due east of Naivasha. During 2012, this area was home to just over 300 individuals.

Nature Kenya and the local site support group, Friends of Kinangop Plateau, have established a small nature reserve to protect several pairs of Sharpe's Longclaw. A visit is highly recommended in order to observe this very special bird and learn more about the problems it faces. This can be a very difficult species to find without local knowledge and I recommend that you make contact with the best local guides around Murungaru whose details can be found at the rear of this book.

Sharpe's Longclaw was named in honour of Richard Bowdler Sharpe (1847–1909), a British zoologist and assistant keeper of the British Museum's vertebrate section, who was a prolific author and founder of the British Ornithologists' Club in 1892.

Sharpe's Longclaw (17 cm | 6½") can be told from the similar Yellow-throated Longclaw (*page 119*) by its smaller size and the lack of a black band on the side of its throat and breast.

Woodland, scrub and garden

This section covers the birds of woodland, scrub and gardens, all habitats that could be summed up by one word – 'leafy'. However, as 'leafy' vegetation also occurs on many cliffs in the Rift Valley, those cliff-dwelling species that require this vegetation 'type', such as the two **'red-winged' starlings** and the **Little Rock Thrush**, are also included within this habitat section.

Woodland

Trees require plenty of fresh water and there are therefore two places where rich woodlands should and do occur: where there is high rainfall; and close to a body of fresh water. As explained previously in the grasslands section, higher altitude areas receive the highest rainfall and the richest woodlands tend to be found in the highest parts of the Rift Valley, between Lakes Naivasha and Nakuru. There are, however, trees surrounding most of the lakes in the Rift Valley and even the edge of saline Lake Bogoria is well-wooded. The exception is Lake Magadi where the especially saline water is not conducive to tree growth.

The tallest and most impressive woodlands are the 'fever forests' that are found around Lakes Naivasha and Nakuru. These contain large specimens of the Yellow-barked Acacia, or Yellow Fever Tree, that are rich in birdlife, including **Olive Pigeon** and the **helmetshrikes**.

Scrub

In areas that do not support woodland, a wide variety of low trees, shrubs and other plants may persist to create scrub, which often forms an impenetrable tangle. This provides a perfect habitat in which many birds, including the **babblers** and numerous **warblers**, feed and nest.

Gardens

Many visitors to the Rift Valley will spend quality time in dedicated tourist accommodation, of which there is a wide variety on offer. Some of the finest safari lodges and luxury camps in East Africa have been established in the Rift Valley and there are also many humble digs and basic campsites. However, one thing they have in common is that they ALL have a garden, of some size or another, which will attract a surprising number of bird species. Regardless of where you sleep on the luxury-to-basic spectrum, an early morning bird-walk is guaranteed to get your day off to a good start. Here are a few useful pointers to help you on your way:

- Watch out for flowering aloes that will attract the local sunbirds.
- Find out if there is a bird-feeding table. If there isn't one, take some bread and whistle some birds in – they will come!
- Visit a place where water is available for birds to drink and/or bathe, especially in dry areas.
- Learn a different bird song or call each time you go out – just watch and listen.
- Watch out for ant trails. Although care is needed as certain ants can bite, ant swarms are a particularly attractive food source for some bird species, including woodpeckers.

Rich in colourful aloes and grasses, the gardens of Sunbird Lodge, overlooking Lake Elementeita, are just as rich in birdlife.

The dry, acacia-dominated scrub surrounding Lake Baringo.

Owls and **nightjars** are nocturnal and can be very difficult to observe. Unless you make a concerted effort to find them during the daytime, you are most likely only to have a quick glance at a bird in the car headlights. But there are measures you can take to ensure that you find these special birds:

- Walk with a local guide or someone who knows a particular site very well – local knowledge cannot be beaten. At Lake Baringo, in particular, there are plenty of excellent guides who can show you owls and nightjars, as well as other wildlife. Do try to keep your noise level down to avoid disturbance as the birds may be nesting and will, at the very least, be trying to rest.

- Listen at night and early morning for owls in the area. Most owls and nightjars have distinctive calls that can be easily recognized, especially if you purchase a good collection of bird sounds for reference (see the section on *Useful resources page 244* for suggestions). Tracking a call early in the morning can help you to find roosting owls during the day.

- In some areas, night-drives may be permitted and it is worth checking with your lodge or camp to find out more. Drive slowly at night as nightjars often land on tracks and roads to keep themselves warm and can be easily run over or hit. Owls can often be found perched on roadside poles and fence-posts.

Spotted Eagle Owls are sometimes seen on tracks and roads at night.

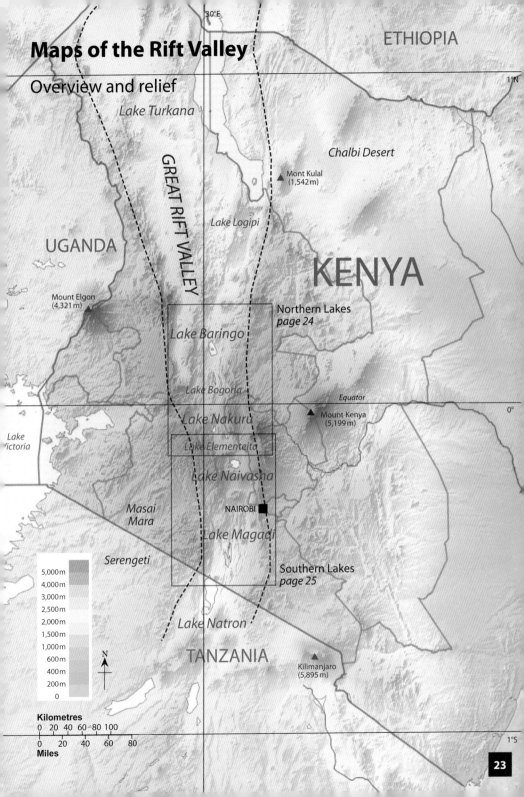

Maps of the Rift Valley

Overview and relief

ETHIOPIA

30°E

1°N

Lake Turkana

Chalbi Desert

▲ Mont Kulal
(1,542 m)

GREAT RIFT VALLEY

Lake Logipi

UGANDA

KENYA

Mount Elgon
(4,321 m) ▲

Northern Lakes
page 24

Lake Baringo

Lake Bogoria

Equator

▲ Mount Kenya
(5,199 m)

0°

Lake Nakuru

Lake
Victoria

Lake Elementeita

Lake Naivasha

*Masai
Mara*

NAIROBI ■

Lake Magadi

Southern Lakes
page 25

Serengeti

5,000 m
4,000 m
3,000 m
2,500 m
2,000 m
1,500 m
1,000 m
600 m
400 m
200 m
0

Lake Natron

N
↑

TANZANIA

▲ Kilimanjaro
(5,895 m)

1°S

Kilometres
0 20 40 60 80 100

0   20   40   60   80
Miles

Maps of the Rift Valley
Northern Lakes

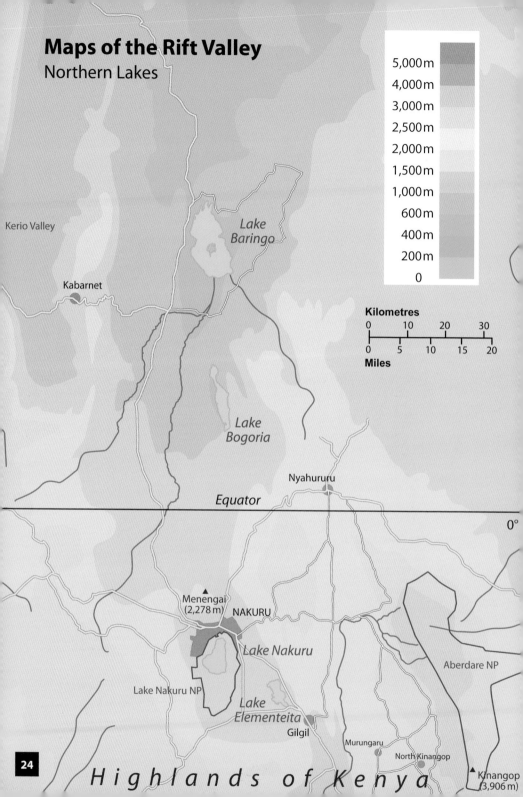

5,000 m	
4,000 m	
3,000 m	
2,500 m	
2,000 m	
1,500 m	
1,000 m	
600 m	
400 m	
200 m	
0	

Kilometres
0   10   20   30

0   5   10   15   20
Miles

Kerio Valley

Kabarnet

Lake Baringo

Lake Bogoria

Nyahururu

Equator   0°

Menengai
(2,278 m)   NAKURU

Lake Nakuru

Lake Nakuru NP

Lake Elementeita

Gilgil

Murungaru

North Kinangop

Aberdare NP

Kinangop
(3,906 m)

H i g h l a n d s   o f   K e n y a

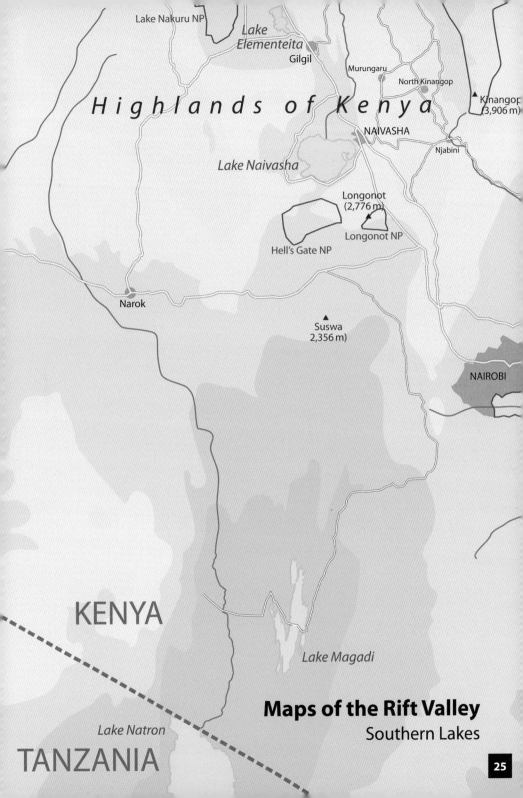

Lake Nakuru NP

Lake Elementeita

Gilgil

Murungaru

North Kinangop

▲ Kinangop
(3,906 m)

H i g h l a n d s   o f   K e n y a

NAIVASHA

Njabini

Lake Naivasha

Longonot
(2,776 m)

Longonot NP

Hell's Gate NP

Narok

▲
Suswa
2,356 m)

NAIROBI

KENYA

Lake Magadi

Maps of the Rift Valley
Southern Lakes

Lake Natron

TANZANIA

General notes: East Africa is host to two of the world's eight pelican species. Both have different feeding strategies but rely on their huge bills, equipped with an expandable pouch, to catch fish. With their large, webbed feet, pelicans are great swimmers and you may notice that they sit high in the water for such bulky birds. This is because air sacs secreted under the skin help to maintain excellent buoyancy. Despite their great size pelicans are fantastic fliers and routinely commute over 100 km in search of feeding grounds, sometimes soaring 2–3 km above the ground. Both species are colonial breeders and gatherings of the noisy, fluffy white young form substantial crèches at breeding sites. At Lake Naivasha, both species are threatened by excessive water abstraction and rising toxicity levels due to the ever-expanding horticultural industry.

☐ **Great White Pelican**

175 cm | 70" (wingspan 290 cm | 115")

A huge, white waterbird with a bright yellow bill. Large flocks of this impressive bird gather in the Rift Valley, especially at Lake Nakuru where groups are very approachable as they loaf and preen along the water's edge. When feeding, groups gather in circles and plunge their mighty bills into the water in unison, creating quite a spectacle. Breeding birds develop a semi-erectile crest and the facial skin colour changes from the usual yellow to orange. The overall plumage of such birds turns quite peachy, so be careful not to confuse this species with the Pink-backed Pelican which, strangely, looks less pink than a breeding Great White! It only breeds on rocky islands on Lake Elementeita, but not every year. Young birds are able to fly after 3 months, when their plumage is still very brown, and may take 3 years to reach maturity.

The Great White Pelican is the national bird of Romania.

Great White Pelican
The black flight feathers contrast strongly with the rest of the plumage, which is white.

Pink-backed Pelican
The slightly darker flight feathers show little contrast with the off-white body, making in-flight identification quite straightforward.

☐ **Pink-backed Pelican**
150 cm | 60" (wingspan 240 cm | 96")
A large, greyish waterbird with a dull-coloured bill. This is the smaller of the two East African pelicans. It is less numerous than the Great White Pelican and does not engage in group-feeding activities. The Pink-backed Pelican nests colonially in trees and breeding birds acquire a yellowish bill and paler body plumage, but this is never as bright as the Great White Pelican's and stays fairly drab for much of the year. It also acquires a comical shaggy crest during the breeding season. Despite the bird's name, it can be very difficult see the 'pink back' at any time during the year.

Breeding

Non-breeding

27

☐ **African Darter** 79 cm | 31"

A snake-necked bird of quiet waters. While built on a similar frame to the cormorants, the African Darter is a far more refined bird with an air of elegance about it. It has a long, slim neck and sharp bill that is used to spear fish like a harpoon – and it is not uncommon to see a bird rise from an underwater dive with a fish impaled on the end. Darters often swim on the surface with their backs submerged and can be difficult to find when just the long neck and head are exposed. At the breeding grounds, such as Lake Baringo, pairs nest in the company of herons and egrets. Young birds are white and fluffy.

Great Cormorant

Reed Cormorant

African Darter

Reed Cormorant 53 cm | 21"

A dark, duck-sized bird of open waters. Considerably smaller than the Great Cormorant, this bird is also much smaller in its proportions, with the exception of having a comparatively longer tail (and hence is often referred to as Long-tailed Cormorant). Adults are dark-necked and immatures much paler, while breeding adults sport a short crest above the bill. Although less obvious than the Great Cormorant, this bird is numerous and widespread across the Rift Valley lakes.

▼

Great Cormorant 100 cm | 40"

A pied, goose-sized bird of open waters. There is great variation in the plumage of these thickset waterbirds: some adults are white-breasted, whereas others are mostly black with a white chin. However, when in breeding plumage, all show a large white patch on the thigh. Immature birds are usually off-white on the entire underside. With the benefit of impressive webbed feet, they are excellent swimmers and their diet consists almost entirely of fish caught underwater. Flocks of these cormorants are often seen following feeding parties of Great White Pelican (*page 26*), chasing fish that they flush. Various races of Great Cormorant can be found across Africa, Asia, Europe, Australia and the eastern seaboard of North America.

◀

In parts of the Far East, particularly in China, people use tethered cormorants to catch fish for their own consumption.

Great White Egret

Little Egret

Yellow-billed Egret

☐ Yellow-billed Egret 70 cm | 27"

A medium-sized, white heron with a yellow bill. Also known as Intermediate Egret, this bird is indeed intermediate in size between the larger Great White Egret and other smaller species, such as Cattle Egret. However judging size is only really possible when the different species are close by. Instead, try to base your identification on two other features – the gape and the neck. The gape is the line that runs from the bill opening and in this species does not extend beyond the eye (unlike Great White Egret). The neck is obviously elongated and shows at least one kink, quite unlike the Cattle Egret (*page 32*) which is invariably hunched most of the time and does not show a kinked neck. The leg colour changes from yellow to black in the breeding season but never has the mixed colour combination of Little Egret. Like all other egrets, the neck is recoiled backwards in flight.

☐ Little Egret 64 cm | 25"

A medium-sized, white heron with a slim, black bill. The Little Egret is a delicate bird sharing many similarities with the larger Great White Egret but always shows black legs with bright-yellow feet. Also, the black bill contrasts with a yellow patch of skin in front of the eyes and a good view will usually reveal a long, elegant crest. This species has a rarely seen 'dark morph' plumage that is slaty-grey all over except for a white chin but beware of similar dark herons such as Western Reef Heron and Dimorphic Egret (*neither shown*) that are scarce wanderers to inland waters.

Great White Egret 92 cm | 36"

A large, elegant and long-necked white heron that is
rarely seen far from water. Although the largest of the
white egrets, confusion with other species is possible,
especially the Yellow-billed Egret. By far the most
reliable feature to separate these otherwise similar
species is the length of the gape (the visible line
that runs from the bill opening), which extends
well behind the eye in this species. As with other
egrets, the plumage varies slightly according to
the time of year. Birds in breeding plumage show
a greenish patch of skin at the base of a black bill,
long white plumes flowing from the back and
breast, and yellowish legs. Non-breeding birds
have an all-yellow bill, blacker legs and lack
the elegant white plumes.

▶

Egrets derive their
name from the
French word *aigrette*,
meaning brush, on
account of the long
filamentous plumes
they acquire in the
breeding season.

Breeding

Cattle Egret

Squacco Heron
Non-breeding

Little Egret
(for comparison)

Cattle Egret

Cattle Egret 56 cm | 22"

A small, short-necked, white egret that associates with grazing animals. Often found in open areas such as grassy plains and arid pasture, where they feed among herds of wild Cape Buffalo or domesticated livestock, these egrets will routinely visit rivers and marshes in order to preen and roost. It is here where they may be confused with other egrets that are associated with water, but this is the only egret that habitually gathers in large flocks. Cattle Egrets have far shorter necks than the other egret species (*pages 30–31*) and are usually seen hunched when roosting. In breeding plumage, birds develop bright-orange tones to the crest and chest, and the facial skin turns bright-red. At this time, the legs are orange, while non-breeding birds show black legs and all-white plumage.

Look out for flocks of Cattle Egrets gathering at the feet of Buffalo, where they feed on invertebrates disturbed by the mammals; they are also often seen riding on the backs of buffalo and other large grazing animals.

Striated Heron 40 cm | 15¾"

A small, dark heron of the lake edge. Its body plumage is mostly grey but it shows pale feather edges, subtle white stripes in the face and a black cap that is erected when the bird is excited or agitated. In the breeding season, its legs change from yellow to pink. Immature birds are similar but heavily streaked on the throat and spotted on the back and wings. In flight, the short yellow legs are obvious, and this is when you are most likely to hear its call – a short, sharp, barking growl.

Non-breeding

☐ Squacco Heron 46cm | 18" ▼

A small, pale heron of marshy areas. Common along the edges of freshwater in the Rift Valley, the Squacco Heron appears short and bull-necked. In breeding plumage, birds are beige with long, cinnamon plumes down the back and a series of black and white plumes emerging from the neck. Immature and non-breeding birds are typically more streaky and have a darker brown back. In flight, birds of all ages show snow-white wings and tail that contrast with the browner colouration of the back. It breeds regularly at Lake Baringo and sporadically elsewhere.

Breeding

Non-breeding

Usually encountered in a hunched position, the Striated, or Green-backed Heron, is a shy bird that prefers keeping to cover around water.

Grey Heron   100 cm | 39"

A large, white-and-grey heron of open water and
marsh. Adult birds are easily identified by their
whitish head, neck and belly, and sport long, black
feathers that extend from above the eye down the
back of the neck. Immature birds show more grey
in the face and lack the adults' black facial plumes.
In flight, birds show darker flight feathers on the
upperwing, while the underwing is uniform grey
with no contrast. An accomplished fisherman, the
Grey Heron is not beyond taking other prey such
as reptiles, young birds and small mammals.
The commonly heard call is a loud "*fronk*".

▶

Immature

Adult

Grey Heron

Black-headed Heron

Black-crowned
Night-heron

☐ Black-headed Heron
92 cm | 36"

A mostly dark, medium-sized heron of marshes and plains. Smaller and darker than the Grey Heron, this species shows a white throat that contrasts markedly with the darker head and back of the neck. In flight, the upperwing is darker than in Grey Heron and the underwing shows an obvious contrast between the white coverts (front half of wing) and blackish flight feathers (back half of wing). Although fond of open marshes like other herons, the Black-headed Heron is frequently seen walking in grassy areas in search of frogs, lizards and snakes. It has an unrushed approach to killing snakes and it is not uncommon to see the snake wrapping itself around the bird's bill – making for spectacular wildlife viewing!

◀ ☐ **Black-crowned Night-heron** 60 cm | 24"

A pale, hunched nocturnal heron. As the name suggests, this bird is primarily a nocturnal feeder but can be found during daylight hours. It prefers to spend most of the day sleeping in trees and bushes in loose groups (often in Yellow-barked Acacia), when its hunched silhouette is often all that can be seen. When adults are out in the daytime, they are easy to identify. However, immature birds, which are dark brown and heavily spotted, could be confused with immature Striated Heron (*page 33*) but that species is much smaller. The best time to see these birds is during the hour before sunset when they begin to emerge from their roosts and fly to feeding areas, looking very pale-winged as they do. Night-herons give a loud, growling "*quark*" when disturbed.

The Goliath Heron is the largest heron in the world and named after the biblical giant defeated by David.

Hamerkop 56 cm | 22"

The Hamerkop (Dutch and Afrikaans for Hammer Head) is an oddity among African herons because of its all-brown colour, peculiar 'hammer-head' and short legs. Like other herons, it is an accomplished fisherman and is often seen at the water's edge waiting for frogs and fish to come within striking distance. Other feeding tactics include wiggling its feet in mud to stir up food items, and flying into the wind, close to the water, dipping at the surface to pick off fish. The Hamerkop's nest is built in a strong tree, and is added to each year. These extended constructions offer 'apartments' for other birds, such as sparrows and weavers. Abandoned Hamerkop nests are frequently taken over by a variety of species, including raptors.

A Hamerkop's call, usually given in flight, is a high-pitched "*chink-chink, chink*" that sounds like a hammer striking an anvil. This is why the bird acquired its local name of 'fundi chuma', the blacksmith.

▼

Goliath Heron

Hamerkop

Purple Heron

▼ ☐ **Purple Heron** 85 cm | 34"

A slim, chestnut-headed and grey-backed heron of lakes and quiet waters. Although similar in plumage to the Goliath Heron, which appears huge and powerful, this neat heron always looks slim and elegant. It also shows more extensive black streaking on the face and neck than the Goliath Heron and has a paler bill that often appears yellowish. It is very much at home in reedbeds and is therefore not always easy to find. In flight, both Goliath and Purple Herons show a rich maroon-chestnut underwing but Purple Heron shows a contrast between the greyish back and darker flight feathers, a feature that Goliath Heron does not show.

◀ ☐ **Goliath Heron** 152 cm | 60"

A huge, chestnut-headed and grey-backed heron of lakes and quiet waters. With its huge, dagger-shaped bill and gigantic proportions, this really is an impressive bird by anyone's standards. In flight, look out for the rich-chestnut underwing and very broad wings. In the Rift Valley, it could be confused with the similar-looking Purple Heron but is much bigger in both size and proportions. Take time to enjoy this bird fishing and, if it appears to be resting, you may be lucky enough to watch it sunbathing, when it stands facing the sun with its wings held half-open.

Adult

Immature

37

Abdim's Stork 81 cm | 32"

A mostly black stork with a colourful face.
Like the scarce Black Stork, the Abdim's Stork
is a non-breeding migrant that arrives from
October to April but unlike that species it
may descend in thousands. It breeds in
central Africa where it is considered a
good luck symbol and bringer of the rains.
Like other grassland storks, this bird walks
endlessly in search of grasshoppers, locusts,
small reptiles and amphibians. Abdim's Stork
is the smallest of all true storks and shows
a conspicuous white belly in flight as well
as a white rump, which easily separates it
from the dark-rumped Black Stork.

Named after the Governor of Wadi Halfa,
Ben El-Arnaut Abdim, a Turkish civil servant
working in Sudan from 1821 to 1827, who
assisted Rüppell (of Rüppell's Vulture fame,
page 90) during his collecting expeditions in
North Africa.

Black Stork 102 cm | 40"

A large, glossy black stork. Often
encountered alone and rarely in
numbers exceeding five, the Black
Stork is a handsome bird. Adults
show a long, bright-red bill and
eye-ring, both of which appear
duller on immature birds, and the
plumage is black with a colourful
oily iridescence. Like Abdim's
Stork, this bird shows a white belly
but lacks the white rump of that
species. Unlike the popular White
Stork (*page 40*), which nests on
rooftops in towns across southern
Europe, this bird is more reclusive,
preferring instead to nest in forests
and on cliffs.

Abdim's Stork

Black Stork

☐ African Open-billed Stork
81 cm | 32"

An all-dark stork with a large bill. These are non-breeding seasonal wanderers that arrive in vast flocks, sometimes numbering thousands, when the marshes are wet. They are specialist snail-feeders that use their stout bills, which show an obvious gap near the tip, to crack open the shells like a set of nutcrackers before manoeuvring the soft mollusc down the throat. In flight, flocks soar on flat wings, when they bear an uncanny resemblance to a prehistoric pterodactyl! The closest breeding colonies are on Lake Victoria but our visiting birds are more likely to arrive from larger colonies across central Africa.

Although the bill shape is unique among African storks, there is also an Asian Open-billed Stork found across India and south-east Asia.

White Stork 122 cm | 48"

Distinctive black-and-white storks of long grass plains. These birds are non-breeding migrants from Europe that usually arrive during October and depart in April, although a few birds have been known to stay in southern Africa to breed. Their movements are dependant upon the rains and the water levels within the Rift, but after re-fuelling from a long journey many birds will continue onwards to the Serengeti. They frequently gather in vast flocks numbering in excess of 5,000 birds. The superficially similar Yellow-billed Stork has a longer, yellow bill and distinctive red facial skin. In Europe, White Storks are frequently found nesting on the rooftops of buildings and feature in traditional European folklore as the deliverer of babies.

Saddle-billed Stork 145 cm | 57"

A large, pied stork of marshy areas with a huge, red-and-black bill. The name comes from the bright-yellow, leathery 'saddle' on top of the bill. Although these storks are not abundant, they are easy to identify on account of their distinctive plumage. Solitary birds can often be found wading through wet grass searching for frogs and catfish, and it can be great fun watching them tackle larger prey. Males have a dark eye and females a yellow eye, and both have bright-pink 'kneecaps'. Young birds are greyish and their bill is shorter and lacks the colour of an adult. They take two years to reach maturity, during which time they gradually attain their clean black-and-white plumage and yellow saddle.

As with all storks, the White Stork has no syrinx, or vocal cord, which prohibits them from making any calls. Instead, you may sometimes hear them clatter their bills.

Yellow-billed Stork

Saddle-billed Stork

☐ **Yellow-billed Stork** 108 cm | 42"

A distinctive pied stork with a bare, red face and long, yellow bill. This is a common resident of open marsh and rivers, usually seen resting in a hunched position or wading in shallow water in search of prey. It hunts a variety of aquatic creatures by moving its bill slowly in the water until it feels a food item. The bill is then snapped shut and the prey swallowed. This bird is not beyond piracy and regularly cajoles small herons and egrets into giving up their well-earned fish! In flight, they appear mostly white but have black flight and tail feathers and long, pink legs that extend well beyond the tail.

▼

Look out for the distinctive wing pattern in flying adult birds which look very graceful.

☐ African Spoonbill

91 cm | 36"

A white, stork-like bird with a spoon-shaped bill. Although spoonbills are wacky-looking birds, their strangely shaped appendage really does serve a useful purpose. Often seen feeding in tight groups of five or more, they move fast through shallow water swaying their head from side to side with the bill held slightly apart. When a prey item is felt the bill snaps shut. Spoonbills feed mainly on small shrimps and other invertebrates but sometimes a fish is caught and tossed down the throat. Adults show a red face mask and a greyish bill edged in red, while immatures lack the red colouration. In flight, they hold their neck outstretched.

African Spoonbill

Marabou Stork

RECORD BREAKER Some large individuals have a wingspan in excess of 3·5m (10 feet), making this species, together with the Andean Condor of South America, the longest-winged of all land birds.

☐ **Marabou Stork** 152 cm | 60"

A huge, ugly stork. This bird is best known as a scavenger at the carcass, where it will often wait for the more aggressive vultures to have their fill before stepping in to clean up the scraps. The head is mostly featherless, enabling it to get deep into the carcass without getting blood over its plumage – bare skin being easier to keep clean than feathers. You may also encounter it scavenging around picnic sites at various locations in the Rift, and when lakes start to dry out you can guarantee that Marabou Storks will be in attendance to mop up any floundering fish – the timing of their arrival being uncannily impeccable. Unlike other storks that fly with their necks outstretched, the Marabou carries its head against its body like a heron.

In many parts of Africa, the Marabou is known as the 'undertaker' on account of its habit of opening its wings over a carcass as though measuring it up for a coffin!

☐ **Greater Flamingo** 145 cm | 57"

A very tall flamingo with a bi-coloured bill. These birds have incredibly long necks in relation to their body size and, although always taller than Lesser Flamingo, there is a huge variation in size between the taller males and females. The best feature for separating this species from Lesser Flamingo is the colour of the bill, which is pale pink at the base and black at the tip. When the bird is on the ground, the plumage appears very pale pink apart from the upper parts of the wings that are bright crimson-pink. Immature birds of both flamingo species are greyish-white. Birds in the air show a two-tone 'crimson-black' wing-colour combination. Both species call a goose-like "*honk*".

Two of the world's six flamingo species inhabit Africa. The main nesting site for both flamingo species is Lake Natron, in the north of Tanzania, where over half a million nests can be occupied. Both species lay a single white egg on a raised mud mound and young hatch with a straight bill, rather than kinked as in the adults.

The Greater Flamingo is the state bird of Gujarat, India.

Lesser Flamingo

Greater Flamingo

The Phoenix and the whale: In much the same way that baleen whales filter plankton, flamingos filter a protein-rich soup of mud, salt-water, algae and invertebrates using a specialized tool that is unique to the family. Within the bill are rows of bristles, called lamellae, which are used in conjunction with the rough tongue to extract the food items that pass through it, such as blue-green algae, brine shrimps and tiny molluscs. Carotenoid proteins are extracted from this diet by liver enzymes and it is these that give the flamingo its fabulous pink colouration. The scientific genus for the Greater Flamingo, *Phoenicopterus*, translates from Ancient Greek to 'crimson-wing' but you may also detect from this name the Phoenix, a mythical creature that seems to have been inspired by the flamingo.

■ Lesser Flamingo
90 cm | 36"
A short flamingo with an all-dark bill. With its proportionately thicker neck, this flamingo is not just substantially shorter than the Greater Flamingo but is also less spindly in its overall appearance. Although there is considerable variation between individuals, adults of this species are generally much pinker than Greater Flamingo but, if seen well, it is the all-dark bill that is the best identification feature. In flight, birds show a three-tone colour combination of crimson-white-black in the open wings.

45

Sacred Ibis 73 cm | 29"

A wandering bird of the wetlands that can sometimes be seen in flocks of 20 or more. The general impression of an ibis is that it has a rather 'horizontal' posture, especially in comparison to the 'vertical' storks and herons that they superficially resemble. They are generally active feeders and will walk around wet and grassy areas probing their thick, strongly decurved bill in search of frogs, fish and invertebrates. The head of adult birds is jet-black and lacks feathers, but immature birds can show some white mottling on the face and neck. In flight, birds often show bare, red skin along the front of the underwings, making them appear quite prehistoric.

The bird acquired its 'Sacred' name on account of its religious status among the Pharaohs of ancient Egypt who worshipped the bird in the form of the God they named Thoth. In Saqqara, in one excavated tomb alone, 1,500,000 mummified ibises were discovered!

▼

Glossy Ibis 65 cm | 26"

A quiet brown ibis of lake and marsh. Unlike the noisy Hadada Ibis, that is quite at home in gardens and close to people, the Glossy Ibis is a shyer bird that rarely strays far from water. It is much slimmer and darker brown than the Hadada Ibis and its legs are proportionately much longer. This bird may form sizeable flocks on Rift Valley lakes and they fly in a tight formation, rather like ducks. A close look at the plumage in good light reveals beautiful iridescent feathers on the wings.

▼

Sacred Ibis

Glossy Ibis

■ **Hadada Ibis** 82 cm | 32"

A noisy brown ibis of marshes and wooded open gardens. The bird gets its name from the very loud calls that are usually the first clue to its presence – a raucous "*haa-hahaa*", or sometimes a single drawn out "*haaaaa*". On first impression, the bird can appear a bland brown, but sit and watch and the sunlight reflecting off the wings may reveal a stunning glossy sheen of blue, green, purple and copper; this can often be seen clearly when the bird is in flight. Like the other ibis species, Hadada spend much of their time walking and probing for food. Adult birds show a whitish eye and a pale moustache extending from the red-topped bill.

▼

These birds are very much at home in the company of people, and across southern Africa are commonly found in gardens and parks.

Grey Crowned Crane 110 cm | 43"

Very attractive birds of moist grasslands and marshes. The crown of fine, golden feathers sits on a black, velvety forehead, and below the clean white face disc hangs a red wattle. Although sometimes seen in large flocks, these birds are more often encountered in pairs, walking sedately and feeding by pecking at seeds. If very lucky, you may see them break into a joyous, hopping display dance, which is a fabulous sight to enjoy. Pairs build a floating nest in a shallow pool and rarely lay more than two eggs. The chicks are yellow and rather cute, though immature birds are quite scruffy. The call is a loud honking "*hu-wonk*" that is often given in flight, when they also show large white patches on the forewing.

This is the national bird of Uganda, and are 'grey' and 'crowned' rather than 'grey-crowned'. The distinction is made because there is also a Black Crowned Crane found in West Africa.

☐ Fulvous Whistling Duck
50 cm | 20"

An attractive brown duck that is structurally very similar to its close relative the White-faced Whistling Duck. The plumage is very subtle and understated although the white plumes on the flanks are rather ornate. Often seen at rest during the day, this species is most active at night, when the two-note whistle can be heard. Although this species can be seen in the Rift throughout the year, it does not breed locally and most are visitors from southern Africa.

☐ White-faced Whistling Duck 48 cm | 19"

A gregarious brown waterfowl with a white face. Usually encountered in small flocks, this medium-sized, upright duck is at home along the grassy margins of open marsh and quiet backwaters, but less so on open water where it typically flies if disturbed. These ducks have a very distinctive call, a high-pitched and sweetly whistled "*wer-wi-wooo*", which you are likely to hear before you see the bird. They are long-necked and long-legged, and a good view will present no identification problems. When watching birds in flight, check the colour and pattern of the rump which is dark in this species but shows an obvious white crescent on the Fulvous Whistling Duck. The sexes look similar in both species.

The term 'fulvous' means yellowish-brown.

Whistling ducks are sometimes called tree ducks in the Americas. However, their scientific name *Dendrocygna* means 'tree swan' – all rather confusing considering that they are actually more closely related to geese than either ducks or swans!

49

☐ Spur-winged Goose
100 cm | 39"

An unmistakable large, pied goose with a white face and pink legs. This is a regular visitor to green and flooded grasslands, especially at Nakuru. The black on the back and neck appears glossy green in strong light, contrasting heavily with the white belly. At close range, look out for the warty face of the male and a fleshy red knob on the forehead. In flight, the black upperwing has a white leading-edge and the underwing shows black flight feathers against white. Often calls in flight, a hiccup-like "*ku-wup-up*".

The Spur-winged Goose is not popular among hunters on account of its bad-tasting flesh.

▶

☐ Knob-billed Duck
male 76 cm | 30"; female 56 cm | 22"

A medium-sized pied waterfowl with a white neck. The strange appendage after which this species is named, is only found on the bill of male birds and swells during the breeding season. Although the sexes are otherwise similar, there is a substantial size difference between them, with females on average one third smaller than males. In flight, the wings appear all-dark from above and below unlike the similar Spur-winged ▶ Goose that shows a great deal of white under the wing and on the leading edge.

☐ Egyptian Goose ▶
74 cm | 29"

A common, light-brown goose with a dark eye-patch. This attractive bird probably looks its best in flight, when it shows a large white panel on the upperwing and iridescent green inner flight feathers. Despite their rather serene appearance, these geese can be very aggressive and fights are common where territorial incursions occur. Intruders are threatened with open wings in a show of intimidation followed by noisy honking that quickens in excitement.

Egyptian Goose   **Spur-winged Goose**

Female

Male

The frequently seen goslings are soft and downy, patched with brown and white, but turn brown and look scruffy as they age.

51

Red-billed Teal 48 cm | 19"

A brown duck with obvious cream-coloured cheeks.
About the same size as the Cape Teal, this species
can be easily identified by the mostly brown plumage
and dark-brown cap that contrasts with the off-white
cheeks. The red bill with a black line running down
the centre is a useful identification feature, although
the markings can be become obscured when the bird
has been dabbling in mud. In flight, it shows a broad
cream patch at the rear of the wing, unlike both
Cape and Hottentot Teals. This species shows
a greater preference for freshwater lakes than the
other teals but, like the other species shown here,
feeds mostly at night. It is easy to find, roosting
and preening, by day.

Red-billed Teal

Cape Teal

The word 'teal' comes from the blue-green colour of the same name. The male Hottentot Teal is the only resident teal to feature this colour in its plumage, on the inner flight feathers.

☐ Cape Teal 48 cm | 19" ▲
A silvery-grey duck with a pink bill. When seen from a distance, Cape Teal can appear almost uniform in colour but a closer view reveals a delicate, spotted plumage. This attractive species is widespread across the Rift Valley lakes and is more numerous than other ducks on the most alkaline of lakes, such as Bogoria, where it may gather in large non-breeding flocks in excess of 1,000 birds. Like the other teals on this page, the Cape Teal is a 'dabbling' duck that feeds on a variety of plant and invertebrate life, gleaned by dabbling the bill on the surface of the water rather than diving for food.

◀ ☐ Hottentot Teal 36 cm | 14"
A small, brown duck with a dark cap, yellowish cheeks and blue-grey bill. The smallest of the Rift's resident ducks, this teal is also among the darkest. Although the cheeks are pale, like the Red-billed Teal, there is usually an obvious dark smudge at the top of the neck which separates it from that species. Other useful identification features include the blue-grey bill and the underparts tend to be much warmer brown than other teal species. The word Hottentot derives from a colonial term for the Khoi-Khoi people of south-western Africa, from where this species was first described.

☐ Southern Pochard 50 cm | 20" ▼

A large, dark diving duck. This attractive duck is widespread but nowhere common on the Rift Valley lakes. Males are very dark all over and a good view reveals bright-red eyes. Females are a lighter brown and show two white patches on each side of the face, one close to the bill and another extending from the cheek and down the neck. In flight, both sexes show very obvious white patches in the wing.

Male

Female

Male

Female

☐ Northern Shoveler 50 cm | 20" ▲

A conspicuous migrant duck with a huge bill that occurs in the Rift Valley from September to April. Males are big, colourful ducks with a green head, white chest and bright-orange flanks, whilst females are striped and spotted brown and generally rather dowdy. As with other northern 'dabbling' ducks, males moult into a dull eclipse plumage, between September and December, and may show a white crescent in front of the eyes. Both sexes sport a huge piece of feeding apparatus, that big shovel of a bill, that is shuffled from side-to-side through mud and shallow water. It is believed that a Shoveler's bill is more efficient at harvesting food than those of other dabbling ducks. In flight, birds of both sexes show a fabulous light-blue forewing, unlike any other large duck in the region.

Southern Pochard

Yellow-billed Duck

☐ Yellow-billed Duck 60 cm | 24" ▲

A nondescript brown duck with a yellow bill. A common dabbling duck of freshwater lakes, the Yellow-billed Duck is among the most simple of all waterbirds to identify. The head often appears very dark and the bird shows a bright green patch of colour on the inner flight feathers, known as a speculum, which is particularly noticeable in flight. This duck feeds in much the same way as the Northern Shoveler.

It is interesting to note that there is often a large degree of variation between the plumages of male and female ducks that breed north of the tropics, while the sexes of species that breed closer to the equator are generally rather similar.

The legs of grebes are positioned further towards the rear of the bird than with ducks, which means that they stand more erect when on land. This is also when you may catch a glimpse of their huge, lobed toes (not unlike those of a gecko).

Non-breeding

Breeding

Little Grebe 25 cm | 10" ▲

A small and fluffy-reared waterbird. This dainty little bird shows a rich burgundy-coloured face in the breeding season, which changes to a light brown later in the year. It is not uncommon to see the stripe-headed chicks riding on the backs of their parents, especially when they are just a few days old. These birds feed on fish and invertebrates. The call is a high-pitched series of single notes that rise then fall, often referred to as 'chivvying'. This is the commonest of the three grebe species that occur in Kenya and all appear quite weak in flight.

Common Moorhen 36 cm | 14" ▶

A dark, duck-like waterbird of reedy backwaters. Structurally similar to the Red-knobbed Coot, to which it is closely related, the Moorhen is not uncommon but is generally rather retiring and usually seen stalking the margins of lakes and ponds from where it can quickly run to cover. It is a less gregarious bird than the coot except where conditions are exceptionally favourable. Unlike that species, the bill and shield are red with an obvious yellow tip. Other distinguishing features include the line of white feathers along the flanks, and the white feathers under the tail; these are revealed when the bird is walking, frequently flicking its tail. Unlike the coot, the feet are not lobed, indicative of time spent walking rather than swimming.

☐ Red-knobbed Coot 46 cm | 18" ▼

An all-black, duck-like waterbird of open waters. Frequently seen in sizeable flocks, the Red-knobbed Coot is easily identified by the white shield that extends up from the bill – a feature that gave rise to the expression "as bald as a coot". The red knobs, situated at the top of the white shield, are most conspicuous in the breeding season when they appear like raised red berries on top of the head. Like the Little Grebe it has lobed toes. Coots feed on waterweed and a variety of small fish and invertebrates.

☐ Purple Swamphen 46 cm | 18"

A large, blue, chicken-like bird of freshwater marshes. This impressive bird is among the most colourful of all waterbirds but despite its splendour it can be difficult to locate in tall grass and among stands of reeds and papyrus. Although generally a shy bird, some individuals are relaxed and may allow a close approach. Like the Common Moorhen (*page 56*), the Purple Swamphen prefers to walk in search of food and has impressive long toes like the African Jacana, which are an ideal adaptation for spreading the bird's weight when walking on reeds and grasses lying across the water's surface. However, unlike the jacana, the swamphen also uses its feet to grasp bunches of tender reed stems which it proceeds to shred carefully with its robust red bill.

▶

African Jacana 31 cm | 12¼" ▼

An attractive waterbird with incredibly long toes. Commonly known as the Lily-trotter on account of its habit of walking on floating vegetation, especially water-lilies, the African Jacana has an attractive blue bill and shield on the forehead. Its breeding behaviour is particularly strange because the typical roles of the sexes are reversed. The larger females are outrageously flirtatious and frequently mate with several partners. The smaller males are the ones that build the nest, incubate the eggs and rear the young, quite independently of the female. This rare behaviour is known as polyandry. Look out for them in weak fluttering flight when they appear to be 'all-feet'.

▼ ## Black Crake 20 cm | 8"

A shy black bird of the water's edge. These small birds rarely allow prolonged views or a close approach but, if seen well, look out for the bright yellow bill and pink legs. They prefer to hide away in dense vegetation but lucky observers may sometimes see them on the backs of Hippo where they feed on skin parasites. When trying to locate this bird, listen out for the unmistakable call, a muffled giggling, and dove-like "*crroo-crrr-crrr-coo*" coming from the reeds.

☐ Ruff male 30 cm | 12"; female 25 cm | 10"

A common brown wader of open marsh and lakeside. This is among the most numerous of all waders/shorebirds that occur in the Rift Valley, mostly from September to April. When in Kenya, most Ruff look rather plain with a grey-brown back and breast, a white belly and orange legs, but there is considerable variation between immatures, males and females. Males are usually 20% larger and often show more white around the head and brighter-coloured legs, while immatures arriving in September–October are very rusty brown. Most male birds will have reached their breeding grounds in northern Europe, some even within the Arctic Circle, by the time they acquire their stunning breeding plumage. This includes a fabulous 'ruff' of feathers around the neck which is raised to impress females – and is, of course, how the bird acquired its name.

Immature male

Male in breeding plumage

Male in non-breeding plumage

Female (or Reeve)

☐ Common Snipe 27 cm | 10½"

A small, well-camouflaged wader of open, grassy marshes. This beautifully marked bird can be difficult to find as it keeps well-hidden in the vegetation. It may sometimes be flushed from the marsh, rising sharply, and this is when you may hear the characteristic "*sketch*" call which is fast and abrupt, just like the bird in flight. It has a very long bill that it uses to probe for worms and other invertebrates in wet ground. The tip of the bill is surprisingly flexible and can open by an inch when the base is still closed. It is a migrant from the wetlands of Europe and Asia, usually arriving in September and staying until April. The very similar African Snipe (*not shown*) is less common in the Rift Valley, preferring higher altitudes, and is generally darker with an even longer bill.

☐ Greater Painted-snipe

24 cm | 9½"

A beautifully marked wader of wet grassy marsh. However, despite its ornate plumage, the Greater Painted-snipe is among the most difficult of all waders/shorebirds to locate. It has a habit of hiding away in the grass during much of the day, often crouched, and only coming out to feed in late evening, through the night and early morning when fewer predators are active. It is not a true snipe, like the Common Snipe, and is probably more closely related to the African Jacana (*page 59*). Like the jacana, this bird is polyandrous and females have brighter plumage than the males, which are left to rear the young. If you are fortunate enough to locate this bird, watch when it performs a wing-stretch to reveal a stunning array of spots on the wing.

Female

Male

☐ Pied Avocet 43 cm | 17"

An elegant pied wader with an upturned bill. Identification of this attractive species
should be very straightforward. Although long-legged and quite refined, it is a more
solid-looking wader than the Black-winged Stilt, and has blue rather than pink legs,
while in flight it shows much more white on the upperwing. When feeding, it
sweeps its bill from side-to-side with a scything action, collecting invertebrates
as it does so. It tends to be most common on the alkaline lakes
within the Rift, especially at Bogoria and Elementeita
and it frequently nests at Lake Magadi.

▶

☐ Black-winged Stilt
38 cm | 15"
A very long-legged, black-and-white
wader of the water's edge. Needless
to say, their extra-long, rosy-pink
legs explain the name 'stilt' and
enable them to feed in deeper water
than other wading birds of a similar
size. Stilts are quite at
home in both alkaline
and fresh water, where
they can be found wading
gracefully and dipping their
long, thin bill from side to side
or picking insects off grass stems.
In flight, they are not easy to
confuse, the simple plumage of
all-white head and body contrasting
sharply with the black wings – and
those gangly legs extending well
beyond the tail. Immatures are
similar but are browner and
have duller legs. The distinctive
call is a dripping "*kip-kip-kip*". ▶

Black-tailed Godwit 40 cm | 16"

A tall, mostly brown wader with a long, almost straight bill. This migrant from northern Europe and Asia is fairly common on freshwater lakes between September and April, often associating with other migrant waders/shorebirds. The long bill is dark at the tip and paler at the base, and used in a probing motion in shallow water, mud and wet grass. Before birds return to their breeding grounds in spring, you may see them beginning to moult into their breeding plumage, which is a very attractive brick-red colour. In flight, birds show an obvious white flash through the wing, a white rump and a thick black band at the end of the tail.

Pied Avocet

Black-winged Stilt

Black-tailed Godwit

Spotted Thick-knee 44 cm | 17½"

A cryptically patterned wader of dry scrub and bush. Although this species is rarely encountered near water, it has been included in this habitat section to enable easy comparison between the three similar thick-knee species that are most likely to be encountered. It is very obviously spotted and is often found in the shade of bushes. Like the other thick-knees shown here, it is a reluctant flier by day but will readily run from danger. It is primarily nocturnal and calls vociferously at night – a series of staccato "*weoo-weoo-weoo*" notes that rise and then fall.

▶

Senegal Thick-knee 38 cm | 15" ▶

A cryptically patterned wader of the water's edge. Only likely to be encountered on islands within Lake Baringo, where this species has recently become established. It is one of the many 'Baringo Specials' that birders seek there and is a highly prized species that otherwise occurs north of Kenya in a belt running all the way west to Senegal. The differences from Water Thick-knee are subtle but the bill is larger and shows more yellow at the base, and the grey wing-panel, which is easily seen on resting birds, does not show a white bar along the top.

Thick-knees are also known as dikkops across much of southern Africa.

Thick-knees are very spirited birds and show great valour when defending their eggs and chicks against predators, such as huge monitor lizards, by opening their wings and making darting runs to intimidate them.

Water Thick-knee 41 cm | 16" ▲

A cryptically patterned wader of the water's edge.
These birds can be difficult to find as they prefer to sit motionless rather than fly away from danger. If seen well on the ground, look out for the crouched, horizontal posture, large yellow eyes and green legs. Once airborne the open wings show large white patches. Birds become very active after dark and this is when they are most likely to be heard, screaming a long series of excited "*wee*" notes, starting quickly and rising to a crescendo; this sometimes involves several individuals.

☐ Chestnut-banded Plover 15 cm | 6"

A small and brightly banded wader of alkaline lakes. This is a special bird that only occurs on the soda lakes of East Africa (mainly at Lake Magadi, very rarely elsewhere) and at a few locations in south-west Africa. It has a grey back and both sexes show a rich chestnut-orange breast-band that contrasts with the snow-white throat and underparts. Males have a forehead and crown colour combination of white-black-chestnut-grey, while females show just white and grey. As with Kittlitz's Plover, the legs and bill are dark.

☐ Three-banded Plover
18 cm | 7"

A small plover with two – not three – dark bands across the breast. If you are wondering why it is called Three-banded Plover, just remember that the white band between the two black ones also counts! This attractive little wader, with its bright red eye-rings and pink legs, is often very confiding and allows a close approach, especially in muddy roadside pools. It is also common along wet grassy margins and sandy riverbanks where your attention may be drawn to its very high-pitched "*phew-eet*" contact call. When excited it calls a long, muffled "*wi-wi-sher-wir-wirrit*" that sounds rather like a swift.

Female

Male

Kittlitz's Plover 15 cm | 6" ▶

A small, attractive wader of lake shore and short-grass plains. Unlike the similar plovers shown here, Kittlitz's Plover does not have a breast-band but does show a black stripe running through the face. The forehead and throat are white but the underparts are buffy-brown in colour. This plover tends to lead a double life, spending the breeding season on short-grass plains and the rest of the year residing close to edges of lakes.

Named in honour of Friedrich Heinrich Freiherr von Kittlitz (1799-1874), who was not only a great ornithologist and explorer but also a fabulous artist and a naval officer. In addition to travels around North Africa, he also studied the Pacific Rim on a round-the-world journey.

Immature

Common Ringed Plover ▶
20 cm | 8"

A squat, lake shore wader with a single breast-band. This chunky little wader is a migrant from the north and is readily seen along the edges of lakes and marshes from September to April. It is easily told fromsimilar African plovers by the single black band across the breast, a white collar at the back of the neck and short, orange-yellow legs. Immature birds are less well marked than adults.

Adult

General note: these small sandpipers are all seasonal migrants from Europe and Siberia and can be difficult to separate. When observing them, pay particular attention to their calls and the following three features: rump and tail pattern; leg colour; and the degree of contrast between the upperparts and underparts.

◀ ☐ Wood Sandpiper 20 cm | 8"

A refined sandpiper of flooded grass and the margins of lakes and marshes. Wood Sandpipers are far more numerous than Green Sandpipers and are often, but not always, encountered in extended groups. They lack the strong contrast in plumage of the Green Sandpiper primarily because the back and wings are heavily flecked with pale feather edgings and the sides of the belly also carry some soft barring. This combines to give the bird a more streaked and less 'black-and-white' appearance. The bright yellowish-green legs are a very useful identification feature. In flight, the bird shows a pale-grey underwing and a gentle intergrade between the mottled back and the white rump, while the tail shows several narrow soft bars. The monotone call *"chif-if-if"* is a common feature of wet areas throughout much of the year but birds become scarce between May and August when most head north towards the Arctic Circle to breed.

◀ ☐ Green Sandpiper 23 cm | 9"

A stocky sandpiper of quiet waters. The Green Sandpiper is most similar to Wood Sandpiper but is far less gregarious. It shows much greater contrast between the dark back and wings, which have little in the way of flecking in them, and the white belly. The face is usually quite dark, making the white eye-ring very clear if seen well; it lacks the pale eyebrow extending beyond the eye, which is a feature of Wood Sandpiper. Both the bill and the legs are dark and greenish. In flight, birds appear blackish, especially on the underwing, and show a contrasting clean white rump and three to four strong black bars running across the end of the tail. Rising birds call a piercing *"tlu-EET-wit-wit"* that is far more abrupt than the Wood Sandpiper.

◀ ☐ Common Sandpiper 18 cm | 7½"

A small, short-legged, hunched sandpiper with a brown tail and rump. This migrant, occurring commonly between August and May, may be found along boulder-strewn streams and along the edges of larger rivers and lakes. It stands with a horizontal posture and walks with a bobbing action, regularly 'pumping' its rear-end. Unlike the other two sandpipers shown here, the Common Sandpiper's tail projects well beyond the wing-tips. The belly is crisp white with no barring on the flanks, and a white patch cuts up towards the shoulder. It has a low, pulsating flight action with the wings arched slightly downwards. It lacks a white rump and shows a uniform brown colour across the back and down the tail, which is often spread and appears pointed in the centre. The open wing shows a long, narrow white bar down the middle. The call is a very high-pitched long series of *"swee-swee-swee"* notes.

Common Greenshank ▶
32 cm | 12½"

Little Stint 15 cm | 6"

A very small sandpiper of muddy areas. This little wader arrives into the Rift Valley in large numbers in September and is equally at home on fresh and alkaline waters. It is a very busy feeder, prodding its short stubby bill into the mud with a stitching motion. During the northern winter these birds appear mostly cold grey on the head and back, and white underneath but just before they depart for their breeding grounds in the Arctic they acquire a warm reddish plumage including a chestnut wash over the ears.

▼

A medium-sized, elegant wader of the water's edge. This mostly grey-brown sandpiper is very pale on the underparts and usually shows green legs, or 'shanks' – hence its name. The long bill shows a slight but obvious upward curve and becomes darker towards the tip. Greenshanks are energetic feeders and swing their bill from side to side through the water; they will also often run through the shallows chasing small fish and invertebrates. In flight they appear dark above and pale below with an obvious white triangle running up the back. The resonant "*chew-chew-chew*" call is very distinctive and often alerts you to the bird well before you have seen it.

This is the largest of the migratory sandpipers that visit Kenya from northern Europe. It is usually found here from September until April but some birds remain throughout the year.

Non-breeding

Breeding

Marsh Sandpiper 25 cm | 10" ▲

An elegant and leggy migrant sandpiper with a fine, black bill. A close relative of the Common Greenshank, this species can usually be separated by its thinner, needle-like, straight black bill and overall slimmer appearance. Freshly arrived immature birds may sometimes show yellowish legs and a yellowish base to the bill, but the bill is always slimmer than that of the Greenshank. Adults of both species show greenish legs but in Marsh Sandpiper they appear relatively longer and in flight extend much further beyond the tail. Also in flight, both species show an obvious white wedge extending from the tail up the back.

Large plovers within the scientific genus *Vanellus*, including those here and on *pages 74 & 115* are also known as lapwings.

Blacksmith Plover

31 cm | 12¼"

A common pied plover with a white forehead and the only plover to show black cheeks extending to the breast. In flight, it appears mostly grey-and-black and also shows a white rump contrasting with the black tail. The name derives from its call which, like the Hamerkop (*page 36*), sounds like a hammer striking an anvil: "*tink-tink-tink*". It is thought to be declining in some areas due to competition from Spur-winged Plover, which is expanding its range southwards.

Crowned Plover 31 cm | 12¼"

Common and distinctive waders of open areas. It is best identified by the characteristic head pattern (a black-and white skullcap) from which it derives its name. This species also shows a unique wing pattern which makes it easy to separate from other large plovers, either in flight or when wing-stretching – something it often does when a vehicle approaches close-by. These birds draw a great deal of attention to themselves when performing noisy intimidation flights aimed at distracting predators, such as jackals, birds of prey or Southern Ground Hornbills (*page 111*) from their eggs or chicks. If the predator persists, the plovers will often resort to dive-bombing their enemies which can bring them perilously close to danger – so it is always worth watching to see who wins.

☐ **Spur-winged Plover** 28 cm | 11"

A common pied plover with white cheeks and a brown back. This plover is simple to identify because of its bold plumage – so you do not need to worry about seeing the bony spurs on the wings, after which it is named, as these are usually hidden. Even in flight, the white cheeks stand out against the dark breast but, if seen from above, look for the white bar running from the front to the back of the upperwing. Its call is similar to but higher pitched than that of the Blacksmith Plover, birds often getting carried away with excitement, especially when mating.

▶

Spur-winged Plover

Crowned Plover

☐ African Wattled Plover   34cm | 13½"

A large, brown plover with distinctive facial skin. In some respects similar to the pied
plovers on the previous page, the African Wattled Plover lacks the heavy patches of
black and white, and appears uniform brown from a distance. Close inspection reveals a
delicately streaked head and neck, and spectacular yellow wattles hanging from between
the eyes and the bill. This is complemented by a yellow bill tipped with black, and long,
yellow legs. The wattles of male birds are generally longer than those of females but
otherwise the sexes look similar. This plover is less restricted to open water than similar
species and is often at home close to puddles and wet grass. Calling birds usually start
with a prolonged series of high-pitched "*wherp*" notes but when several individuals join
in excitedly it can quicken to "*wit-wit-wit-wu*".

Breeding

Non-breeding

Grey-headed Gull 40 cm | 16"

The common small gull of inland waters. Usually gathering in sizeable flocks, these pale, boisterous birds are equally happy scavenging their food as they are stealing it and this is frequently seen when feeding flocks of Great White Pelicans gather. The gulls will fly just above the feeding party and as the pelicans raise their bills and pouches full of fish, they swoop in to scare or distract them. It is not a wholly successful method but these birds play the odds and usually get away with something. They will occasionally try the same behaviour, known as kleptoparasitism, on herons and cormorants. The grey head is present when the bird is in breeding condition but otherwise it is white with a black smudge or two behind the eyes. The less common Black-headed Gull (*not shown*) from Europe is smaller and paler.

Breeding

Non-breeding

Gull-billed Tern 38 cm | 15"

A large, gull-like tern with a heavy black bill. This is a common migrant to Rift Valley lakes from Europe and Asia and is usually seen in non-breeding plumage (*i.e.* with a dark smudge running through the eye). The less frequently seen breeding plumage is similar but birds show a solid black cap. While the majority of terns are fish-eaters, the Gull-billed Tern is more cosmopolitan in its diet and is particularly fond of crabs, insects and molluscs that it plucks from shallow water or the surface of mud, usually while in flight; it rarely dives.

White-winged Black Tern 23 cm | 9" ▼

A stunning migrant tern that is very easy to separate from Whiskered Tern in breeding plumage but very difficult in non-breeding plumage. Perhaps the most helpful features are that White-winged Black Tern has a small and narrow black bill, very short red legs, a dark leading edge to the wing and often dark inner flight feathers and a few retained black feathers from the breeding plumage. It also shows a white rump and tail in all plumages that usually contrasts with the darker back. This species often gathers in big flocks and hawks over grass for insects and other invertebrates.

Non-breeding

White-winged
Black Tern

Breeding

**White-winged
Black Tern**

Non-breeding

Breeding

Whiskered Tern

Non-breeding

▢ Whiskered Tern   26 cm | 10"

A very attractive resident tern, the Whiskered Tern
is easy to identify in the breeding season due to
the combination of black cap, white cheeks and
sooty-grey belly. It is less easy to identify in non-
breeding plumage as it appears very similar to
a non-breeding White-winged Black Tern.
However, there are a few useful identification
features, particularly the clean leading-edge
to the wing and the lack of an obvious black
'teardrop' behind the eye, just a dark smudge
through the eye that reaches the rear of the crown.
Juveniles are surprisingly easy to identify as they
are rusty-coloured on the back. Birds are most
common on freshwater lakes where they shallow
dive for small fish but they will also hawk over
wet grass to collect insects and larvae.

Breeding

▶

This is the largest
of the world's
93 species of
kingfisher.

▼ ☐ **Giant Kingfisher** 43 cm | 17"

A huge, chequered kingfisher of quiet fresh waterways. Generally scarce and shy, the Giant Kingfisher is about the size of a crow and has a thick, shaggy crest at the back of the head. Males show a chestnut-red breast-band, whereas females have a chestnut-coloured belly. It hunts fish, crabs and amphibians by diving from a perch, often several feet above the water. When encountered on foot it is easily disturbed, calling a loud "*kark*" note as it flies away, but birds are often more approachable during boat trips.

▲

☐ **Malachite Kingfisher** 12 cm | 4½"

A brilliant blue-and-red jewel of still and slow-moving water. Despite its tiny size, the Malachite Kingfisher causes gasps of amazement because of its stunning plumage. Sometimes found balancing from a grass stem hanging over a small pool, it sits and watches for any small fish or tasty morsel to surface, snatching it with a rapid dive. It then proceeds to slam the unfortunate fish on its perch to kill it and to make swallowing it, head first, easier. Otherwise, a flash of brilliant colour whizzing along the water at top speed is the typical view. The nest is made at the end of a long tunnel in a sandbank. The simple call is a soft high-pitched "*peep*".

Pied Kingfisher 25 cm | 10"

A common black-and-white
kingfisher of open water. Regularly
seen hovering over rivers and
marshes, the Pied Kingfisher is quite
unmistakable and not at all shy.
Pairs and family parties are often
seen together and their metallic "*chit*"
contact calls are frequently heard in
unison. Males are easily told from
females by their two solid black bands
across the chest; females show just a
single, broken band. It is among the
most cosmopolitan of all kingfishers,
being found in south-eastern Europe
and across the Middle East and
southern Asia to China, as well as
throughout Africa.

▶

Female

Male

Yellow Wagtail 19 cm | 7½"

A highly variable migrant wagtail. With a breeding range
that covers almost all of Europe and Asia, the Yellow
Wagtail is represented by many regional races, the males
of which all show a distinct head pattern. Variations
include white, yellow, blue, grey and black caps. Females
tend to be plain-faced, but all adults show an olive-green
back and some yellow on the underside. These birds are
attracted to marshes and lake shores, and to feeding
herds of cattle and buffalo, which they follow through
grassland and feed on the insects that are disturbed.
They gather in flocks and
maintain contact with a
loud, high-pitched
"*sreeep*" call.

'Black-headed'

'Sykes's'

'Blue-headed'

'Yellow-headed'

Mountain Wagtail 19 cm | 7½" ▶

A delicate and long-tailed wagtail of wooded streams. In the Rift Valley, this bird is most
easily seen at the Makalia Falls in Lake Nakuru National Park but does occur elsewhere.
Unlike the African Pied Wagtail, it lacks black on the head and back and only shows a
thin, often faint, chest-band. It has the longest tail of Africa's wagtails, the tip of which
is white. Unlike the common migrant Yellow Wagtail, this species lacks any suggestion
of yellow in the plumage but if you should find a wagtail that is otherwise similar to the
Mountain but with yellow under the shorter tail, then you may have stumbled across a
Grey Wagtail (*not shown*), a scarce Palearctic migrant to East Africa.

☐ **African Pied Wagtail** 20 cm | 8" ▼

A small, black-and-white bird with a long tail, commonly found along the edge of rivers. These dainty, strikingly plumaged birds habitually pump their tails when perched and when walking. The frequently heard call is a strong, whistled "*chereep-chup-chup-chup*", sometimes ending "*watcha watcha*". Wagtails are closely related to pipits and longclaws (*pages 118–119*) and all members of this family (Motacillidae) routinely wag, or pump, their tails. Exactly why they do this remains a mystery but studies suggest that it could be a signal of alertness used to deter potential predators. However, wagtails continue to wag even when fully focussed on feeding so it might be a 'fake' signal that continues to work when the bird is 'otherwise engaged'.

Immature

Male

Mottled Swift 21 cm | 8" ▷

A very large all-dark swift with an obvious fork in the tail. Like other swift species, the Mottled Swift can be found over a variety of habitats depending on food availability. It occasionally nests at Hell's Gate National Park and probably at other steep rock faces in the Rift valley.

Alpine Swift 22 cm | 8¾" ▷

A very large swift with a white belly and throat. The largest of all swifts recorded in East Africa, this is also one of the easiest to identify. The breeding grounds are very likely to be on the highest mountains of the region but its movements are poorly understood.

African Palm Swift 18cm | 7"

A uniform, light-brown swift with a long, pointed tail. As its name suggests, this resident species is dependent upon palm trees for nesting and it can often be found hawking for insects in their vicinity. It is common wherever palms are abundant. The long tail often appears fused at the tip but when banking in the air it is frequently spread to reveal a deep notch.

Nyanza Swift 17cm | 6¾"

A dark-brown swift with pale wing-panels. This species appears very similar to the Common Swift but in the fast, active flight, the pale patches on the wings can usually be seen – both from above and below. It is worth noting, however, that the Nyanza Swift is resident in Kenya (breeding mostly in the Rift Valley), and so can be seen year-around (and not just between October and April as with Common Swift). It is often seen in small numbers rather than vast flocks and its call is a trill rather than a scream.

Common Swift 18cm | 7"

A dark-brown swift with a lightly forked tail. A common migrant from Europe and Asia between October and April, the Common (or Eurasian) Swift often arrives ahead of big storms and in huge numbers. Loose flocks can number in excess of 10,000 birds and may take hours to pass overhead – a great example of bird migration that you can actually sit back, admire and enjoy! Like other swifts, they fly very quickly, so getting a good view requires some dexterity with your binoculars. They are generally silent when wintering in Africa, but if you are from Europe or Asia, you may be familiar with their high-pitched screams that herald the arrival of the northern summer.

☐ Little Swift 14 cm | 5½" ▷

A small, dark swift with a white rump. The Little Swift is best separated from the similar Horus and White-rumped Swifts by its very short, square-ended tail that appears round when spread. It is very common around towns and villages where it often forms large, chittering flocks overhead especially as night falls. Birds range widely across a variety of habitats and sometimes swarm over lakes and marshes when insects are hatching. It regularly breeds under the overhangs of solid buildings and makes its nest from feathers and its own saliva. During display, this swift will often find a feather and fly with it in its bill as an invitation to others that it is ready to mate.

☐ Horus Swift 15 cm | 6" ▷

This swift is best described as being intermediate in almost every way between Little Swift and White-rumped Swift and, at first, will probably have you guessing. Perhaps the most useful identification feature is this bird's short tail with a relatively shallow fork. This swift prefers to nest in pre-excavated holes in sandy banks, often next to rivers, that would have been extracted by bee-eaters or martins in the first instance.

☐ White-rumped Swift 15 cm | 6" ▷

A dark swift with a forked tail and white rump. It is separated from Little and Horus Swifts by its much longer, forked tail, although in level flight the fork is not always visible and the tail looks long and pointed. To be sure of your identification, just wait a while until it banks and spreads its tail. Another feature to look out for is a thin white line along the rear edge of the upperwing – known as the 'trailing edge' – which is lacking in Little and Horus Swifts. White-rumped Swifts will often breed on cliffs and under bridges, with or without water running underneath, and make excited trilling sounds as they return to the nest.

Little Swift

Horus Swift

White-rumped Swift

Mosque Swallow 21 cm | 8"

A large, blue-capped swallow with a red rump and orange under the tail. Less numerous than other resident swallows on this page, the Mosque Swallow has never really shown a preference for Muslim places of worship but prefers old trees with suitable nest-holes instead. When flying overhead, look out for the white underwing contrasting heavily with the dark flight feathers.

Red-rumped Swallow
18 cm | 7"

A blue-capped swallow with a red rump and black under the tail. A common breeder in the Rift Valley, often on, in or near to buildings, this swallow shows orange cheeks compared to the white cheeks of the larger Mosque Swallow but is otherwise very similar.

Lesser Striped Swallow
17 cm | 6½"
A chestnut-headed swallow with a red rump and heavily striped underparts. This common resident shows a preference for riverine habitats, frequently nesting under bridges. It is also very much at home in human homes and frequently nests under eaves.

Wire-tailed Swallow 18 cm | 7"
A blue-backed swallow with a chestnut cap and white underparts. This widespread resident breeds close to water, including under bridges, and may also be found nesting in outbuildings, especially at airstrips. The end of the tail is straight (rather than forked) and, in most plumages, shows two prominent stiff and straight outer tail feathers. By far the best identification feature is the clean white throat and belly, which separates it from other blue-backed swallows.

Plain Martin 12 cm | 5"

A brown martin of rivers and lakes. Also known as the Brown-throated or African Sand Martin, this bird is common throughout the Rift. It is mostly sandy-brown all-over but has a whitish belly and a dark, grey-brown throat. It excavates nest holes in sandy riverbanks that are frequently taken over by Horus Swifts (*page 84*) once vacated.

Rock Martin 12 cm | 5"

An all-brown martin with white spots in the tail. Often found well-away from water, the Rock Martin is fond of buildings and cliffs and is quite at home in the company of humans. Unlike all other swallows in the region, it shows no white in its plumage with the exception of the diagnostic spots on the lightly forked tail.

Barn Swallow 19 cm | 7½"

A blue-backed swallow with a red throat and pale belly. Familiar to many visitors from outside of Kenya, the Barn Swallow is a common migrant to Kenya between September and April but stragglers have been recorded throughout the year. Good views of the velvet-red throat and blue breast-band help to separate it from the Angola Swallow (*not shown*), which is a scarce breeder in the Rift. That species shows a reddish-orange throat and light dusky-grey underparts, and lacks the blue breast-band. Young Barn Swallows are less strongly marked than adults and lack the long tail streamers of birds in breeding plumage as do many adults that arrive into Kenya from September onwards.

Banded Martin 15 cm | 6"

A large, brown martin with a broad chest-band. Unlike the other two martins shown here, this charming bird shows a clean white throat and belly and a close view reveals a white comma in front of the eye. It could be mistaken for the smaller Sand Martin (*not shown*), which lacks the eye comma, and both are frequently seen over marshes and grassland.

☐ Rüppell's Vulture 104 cm | 41"

A larger vulture than the similar White-backed Vulture, Rüppell's Vulture is reliably told from that species by its cream-coloured bill at all ages. Adult birds also show obvious pale scalloping to the wing feathers and never a white rump in flight. It nests on remote, precipitous cliffs, such as those at Hell's Gate NP. Being larger than the White-backed Vulture, it can easily use its strength to out-compete that species when similar numbers are present at the carcass, but it is rarely the first to arrive.

This bird is named after the German Wilheim Rüppell (1794–1884) whose zoological and ethnographical collections from North Africa dated between 1822 and 1833.

▼

See *page 244* for some vulture-related weblinks.

☐ White-backed Vulture 98 cm | 39"

The commonest vulture in the Rift. At first glance, many vulture species may appear quite similar but it pays to know 'who is who' when watching these birds at the carcass, as the different species have different feeding behaviours and strategies. White-backs play the 'numbers game', benefitting most when ten or more of its kind are at a carcass, and use intimidation tactics to push other, larger species away. It can be identified by its all-black bill (compare with Rüppell's Vulture) and the plain-brown plumage on the wings. Adult birds appear very pale, almost white, especially in flight when the belly and underwing contrast with the dark flight feathers. The white rump can only be seen from above and rarely when the bird is on the ground. Immature birds are mostly brown all-over, including the rump, but share the black bill of the adult. It nests in tall, mature trees and rarely on cliffs.

▼

Hooded Vulture 75 cm | 30"

A small vulture with a bare, pink head. Generally found in small groups, it is the smallest of the resident vultures in the Rift and is usually seen at the periphery of a carcass waiting for other, larger, vultures to have their fill. The bill is especially slim for a vulture as it is not needed to rip open any skin or flesh; that work has already been done by the time it gets a chance to feed. Instead, it is the perfect tool for tearing at the smaller tendons and scraps often deep inside the remains of the carcass. Adult birds have a pink, bare-skinned face often topped with a 'woolly wig'. Immature birds show darker 'woolly' head feathers and blue skin on the face. In flight, it appears all-dark and the tail is short. Like the White-backed and Lappet-faced Vultures, this bird nests in trees, although very few pairs breed locally.

Lappet-faced Vulture 115 cm | 45"

The king of the African vultures. Its overall size and huge, ivory-coloured bill make this vulture an impressive sight at any carcass – although the saggy, bare-skinned face means that it is perhaps not the prettiest! In flight, the vast, broad wings show a clear white line across the 'arm' and the white 'leggings' can give it a white-bellied appearance. The short tail is obviously wedge-shaped. Immature birds are similar but the face is often less pink and they lack the white 'leggings' of the adult, which become more obvious as the bird reaches maturity at around six years old.

Although this species is far less numerous than White-backed or Rüppell's Vultures, its feeding strategy is simple but successful – sheer size and power – and it will dominate any number of other vultures at the carcass. It prefers to nest in the top of an acacia or desert palm tree.

Immature Adult

Vultures in flight

Identifying vultures in flight can be straightforward if you know what you're looking for...

☐ Hooded Vulture ▶

(*page 91*)
Wingspan 170 cm | 67"

The 'small' one (but still a very large bird). The darkest of the vultures, although adults show a silvery sheen to the base of their flight feathers.

☐ Lappet-faced Vulture (*page 91*)

Wingspan 290 cm | 114"

The 'massive' one. An enormous bird with baggy white 'shorts' and an obvious white bar across the front of the underwing. The large, pink head is usually visible.

▼

◀ ☐ Rüppell's Vulture

(*page 90*)
Wingspan 260 cm | 102"

The 'scaly' one. Look out for cream bars running across the belly and underwing.

☐ **Verreaux's Eagle** (*page 96*)
Wingspan 220 cm | 88"

The 'black' one. A very large and long-tailed
eagle that shows large white panels in the
wing but is otherwise black. Note the odd
shape of the wings with their obvious bulge.

▶

☐ **White-backed Vulture** (*page 90*)
Wingspan 230 cm | 90"

The 'common' one. Adults have a white
underwing contrasting with the darker
flight feathers. Immatures are dark-brown
under much of the wing and
show a white bar near the
front of the wing.

▼

Adult

Immature

93

See *pages 100–101* for raptors in flight

☐ **Martial Eagle** 84 cm | 33" ▼

A massive, powerful eagle of open and wooded areas. The greyish-brown head, back and chest of the adult contrasts with the white belly that always shows large, dark spots. Young birds (see *page 100*) are much whiter and lack the all-dark head. In flight, the underwing appears very dark. Birds are often seen soaring high in search of prey but will also watch for prey from a perch. This is a ferocious predator that is known to kill baboons, antelope and large birds including storks, guineafowl and even other birds of prey. It usually nests on top of a large tree.

Adult

Also look out for this bird perched on telegraph poles and roadside posts, when it can be very approachable.

Augur Buzzard
Light form

African Fish Eagle 73 cm | 29"; Wingspan 225 cm | 90" ▼

A stunning large eagle of lake and marsh. The quintessential sound of African waterways, the loud cry of the African Fish Eagle is never to be forgotten – adult birds throw their necks back energetically as the yelping *"weeoww-ow-ow"* call pierces the sky. The distinctive plumage of adult birds should pose no issues with identification. However, immature birds can appear a strange mix of brown and white patches, and only acquire the classic white head after several years. It is common to see these majestic birds soaring on broad wings over wet areas or perched on a conspicuous branch with water in view.

Augur Buzzard 60 cm | 24"

A common broad-winged raptor. Two distinct colour variations occur, known as light and dark forms, although the light form is most common. Light birds show an all-white throat, breast and belly, whereas dark birds are mostly black all-over. In flight (*page 101*), all birds show white at the base of the flight feathers, and a view of the upperwing reveals a chequered pattern on these same feathers. All adults show a rich-orange tail, although the tail is brown in immature birds. They frequently hover for long periods or just hang in the wind barely moving their wings.

Although the main prey item is fish, these eagles will also take lizards and birds as large as flamingos.

African Fish Eagle

Immature

Adult

Verreaux's Eagle 96 cm | 38"

A large black eagle of cliffs and gorges. This stunning bird of prey feeds almost exclusively on Rock Hyrax, a guinea-pig sized mammal, which it picks off cliff faces after a rapid swoop but it may occasionally tackle small monkeys, gamebirds and small antelope. When not engaged in hunting activities, birds spend a great deal of time perched on cliffs and this is when you may see the white braces that roll over the birds back, however, the white rump is generally only seen with a top view of the bird in flight. The tall cliffs at Hell's Gate and Baringo have traditionally been the best sites to look for this powerful predator.

Steppe Eagle 80 cm | 31"

A large, brown eagle with a big yellow gape. This common migrant from Asia was once considered just a race of the Tawny Eagle but is now treated as a full species that can comfortably be identified in the field. Given a good view, the most reliable identification feature in all ages is the bright-yellow gape that extends from the bill to the far end of the eye; in Tawny Eagle the gape stops below the middle of the eye. Immature birds in flight are even easier to identify as they show a bright-cream line running through the middle of the underwing. Adults are usually very dark brown and many show a blonde patch on the back of the head. This eagle is only likely to be encountered between October and April, when they favour well-wooded areas such as Lake Nakuru National Park.

See *pages 92–93* and *100–101* for raptors in flight

Tawny Eagle 74 cm | 29" ▼

A common brown eagle of open savanna. Tawny Eagles are highly variable in their colouration, with some birds being pale cream and others very dark with rich chestnut tones, but most are a light coffee-brown. The yellow gape extends from the strong bill to just below the eye (compare with Steppe Eagle). Immatures tend to be paler than adults and show thin white lines through the upperwing that are obvious in flight. These resident eagles are both active hunters of small mammals and scavengers.

Pale individual

Dark individual

Adult

Immature

This is a classic scavenger of urban areas that is common in big cities and small villages, although it can sometimes be seen at carcasses with the much larger vultures.

Black Kite
61 cm | 24"
A common dark raptor with a distinctive silhouette in flight (*page 101*): the long wings are typically held with a strong angle at the bend, and it usually shows a noticeable fork in its long tail. In both adult and immature birds, much of the plumage is uniform dark brown. It can be told from eagles by the smaller, yellow bill. The Black Kite has a wide distribution across Europe, Africa and Asia, and some ornithologists consider the birds residing in East Africa to be a distinct species, known as Yellow-billed Kite.

Common Buzzard
50 cm | 20"
A medium-sized brown raptor with a reddish tail. This common migrant from Asia arrives into the Rift Valley in September and spends much of its time perched in open woodland, waiting for prey to pass by, although it also an effective scavenger. Great variations in the plumage occur, with some birds showing a cream-coloured head and others a chestnut wash across the underparts, but the majority are brown-backed and lightly barred below. The tail is predominately reddish on the buzzards seen in East Africa and these birds are often referred to as Steppe Buzzards, which may well be a species in its own right. See image of a bird in flight on *page 101*.

Long-crested Eagle 58 cm | 23"
The only dark-brown raptor with a long crest. This small and compact eagle has a preference for open woodland and its distinctive silhouette may be seen as it perches on top of a tree. It watches patiently before dropping down to prey upon reptiles and small mammals. In addition to the long, floppy crest, its bare parts are bright yellow and it sports short, white 'trousers'. It has a peculiar flapping flight on straight wings, which show a large white patch on the top and lots of white on the underside (*page 101*). The tail is dark with grey bars.

Even in a light wind, look for the floppy crest that looks like a crazy punk hairdo!

Identifying raptors
in flight can be
challenging
but the
following
hints should
help.

Martial Eagle
(*page 94*)
Wingspan 260 cm | 102"
A massive eagle. Adults
show a dark head
and underwing, while
immatures are mostly
pale beneath with light
barring on the tail and
flight feathers.

Immature

Adult

Immature

Adult

Adult

Tawny Eagle
(*page 97*)
Wingspan 190 cm | 75"
A large brown
eagle with a broad,
rounded tail.

Steppe Eagle (*page 96*) Wingspan 210 cm | 84"
Similar to Tawny Eagle but larger. Immatures show a
broad pale stripe running through the wing.

Immature | Adult

■ **Augur Buzzard** (*page 95*)
Wingspan 137 cm | 54"

A round-winged raptor with a short, reddish tail. Dark, light and intermediate forms occur.

Light form | Dark form

■ **Bateleur** (*page 105*)
Wingspan 175 cm | 69"

The uniquely shaped 'bulging' wings are often swept-back and the red tail is very short. Immatures begin very brown all-over but become increasingly mottled with black as they mature.

■ **Long-crested Eagle**
(*page 99*)
Wingspan 120 cm | 48"

A medium-sized blackish raptor with large white panels in the wing and a short barred tail.

■ **Common (Steppe) Buzzard**
(*page 99*)
Wingspan 130 cm | 52"

A brown-bodied, medium-sized raptor with a reddish tail.

■ **Black Kite** (*page 99*)
Wingspan 150 cm | 59"

An all-brown raptor with a distinctive fork in the tail.

All harriers fly with their wings held raised is a shallow 'V' and sometimes appear to float over the ground.

☐ **Pallid Harrier** 46 cm | 18"

Very similar to Montagu's Harrier and even experts struggle to identify some individuals. Identifying males is straightforward: they are very pale grey and white, almost ghostly, but show narrow black patches on the outer wing. Females and immatures are very similar to Montagu's Harrier but the inner flight feathers usually appear blackish in female Pallid Harrier and there is usually a whitish collar visible between the breast and the face. Immatures of both species are warm orange below.

▼

Female (immature)

Male

Pallid Harrier

Male

Montagu's Harrier

Female

Male

Montagu's Harrier is named after Colonel George Montagu (1751–1815), a keen British naturalist and soldier who served in the American Revolution, and who unfortunately died of tetanus after stepping on a rusty nail.

☐ **Western Marsh Harrier** 56 cm | 22" ▼

A distinctive large harrier of marsh and open grasslands. As with the other migrant harriers shown here, there is a significant difference between sexes and immature birds. Males are a rich brown with a pale head and in flight show extensive grey through the wings and tail, and black outer flight feathers. When viewed from below, they appear very pale but the black wing-tips are obvious. Females and immatures are similar, being mostly dark brown all-over with a cream-coloured crown. Females also show a big splash of cream on the front of the wing that is obvious when perched and in flight. Adults of the similar African Marsh Harrier (*not shown*) show a heavily barred tail and underparts and immatures lack the cream crown.

Male

Female

☐ **Montagu's Harrier** 46 cm | 18"

A graceful long-winged bird of marsh and open grasslands. The sexes are very different in appearance, with males mostly grey and females streaky brown. Immature birds are similar to females but show a dark face patch and warm-orange colouration to the underparts and underwing. In the buoyant flight, males show black tips to the wing and a narrow black bar along the middle of the upperwing. The brown females have a whitish belly streaked with brown and a clean white rump patch. Females and immatures of this and similar harrier species are commonly known as 'ringtails'. Montagu's Harrier is a long-distance migrant from Europe and Asia and can usually be found between October and May, often gathering in small numbers to roost, particularly on airstrips.

▢ Dark Chanting Goshawk
56 cm | 22"
A silver-grey raptor of open areas. Often encountered on telegraph poles and posts, this smart bird of prey perches upright on its long, red legs. The soft parts of the bill, known as the cere, are similarly bright red, a feature that separates it from the Eastern Chanting Goshawk (*not shown*) that occurs east of the Rift (that species has a yellow cere). Immatures are dark brown and heavily barred below. It appears very stiff-winged in flight when the black tail, edged and tipped with white, can be seen clearly.

▢ Bateleur 70 cm | 28 cm ▶
The classic soaring bird of the open plain. It shows a distinctive silhouette in flight (*page 101*) with swept-back, angular wings and a tail so short that it sometimes appears to have no tail at all. The chunky, black body and chestnut tail of the adult contrasts markedly with the white underwing, which always shows a black edge to the rear (this is narrow in females and broad in males). Females also show a large, grey band in the flight feathers that can be seen on the upperwing in flight and when perched.

Both sexes have red legs and a bare, red face, while immatures show blue-green bare parts and a uniform brown plumage. The commonly heard call is a gruff "*yaaargh*", which is often followed by rapid flapping of the wings. Prey items include small mammals, reptiles and birds, and it is also an active scavenger.

▢ African Harrier Hawk 66 cm | 26"
An elegant grey raptor of wooded areas with a bare face. Adult birds are mostly grey with white, finely barred underparts. In flight, the long, black tail shows a single white band and the wings are grey and broad with darker flight feathers. The bare facial skin is yellow but this often flushes to bright pink when the bird becomes excited. Immature birds are mostly brown and nondescript. Food items include palm fruits and a variety of reptiles and young birds. Unique among African raptors, the Harrier Hawk has double-jointed legs which enable it to explore nest holes of birds by rotating the talons all the way around. Look out for it flying along the edge of the plain and resting in exposed trees where weavers are nesting. It is commonly known as the Gymnogene in southern Africa.

Bateleur is the French word for acrobat and was given to the bird on account of its habit of tipping for balance in flight, like a tight-rope walker.

Gabar Goshawk 36cm | 14"

A small grey raptor of open scrub and well-wooded areas. Looking very much like the buzzard-sized Dark Chanting Goshawk (*page 104*), this falcon-sized predator makes dashing flights after small birds up to the size of doves. The red bill and legs, together with the finely barred underparts help to separate it from the similar-sized but shorter-tailed Black-shouldered Kite. It shares the long tail of some falcons but is separated in flight by a white rump and much broader, rounded wings that are heavily barred underneath. Immatures are similar but browner and an all-black, or melanistic, morph occurs sporadically in the Rift.

☐ Pygmy Falcon 20 cm | 8"

A tiny, pale raptor of dry scrub. This species is unmistakable given a good view and although the sexes look similar females can be told from males by their brown back. The smallest of all African raptors, this thrush-sized falcon is usually found in the company of White-headed Buffalo Weavers (*page 217*), taking over the maintenance of one of their unused nests in which to rear its own young. There seems to be little conflict between the falcon and the weaver colony and it can only be assumed that the falcon provides them with some level of protection. It feeds primarily on a wide variety of invertebrates, lizards and small mammals that it catches by dropping from a perch.

☐ (African) Black-shouldered Kite 35 cm | 14"

A small, pale raptor of open areas, often encountered perched on top of an acacia.

It appears white below and pale grey above, with a dark patch on each 'shoulder' and a close view reveals bright-red eyes. When perched, notice how the long wings extend beyond the very short, white tail. When searching for prey, such as grasshoppers and small reptiles, it will circle an area of grassland and hover frequently, when it could be mistaken for a Common Kestrel (*page 109*) – although that falcon has a much longer tail. It could also be confused with some male harriers (*pages 102–103*) but they also have much longer tails and wings. The world birding authorities have recently changed this species' name to Black-winged Kite but the old familiar name is retained by the Bird Committee of Nature Kenya.

Male

Female

Lanner Falcon 46 cm | 18"

A large, powerful falcon of cliffs and open areas. The broad, pointed wings and chunky tail are perfect for aerial pursuit. Watching a Lanner chase its prey in mid-air, usually a bird up to a small bustard, in size can be as exciting as seeing a Cheetah in full chase. Occasionally they will attempt to tackle even larger prey, such as small antelope and monkeys.

They appear very pale from below and slate-grey from above. A good view should enable the chestnut patch on the back of the head and smart black moustache to be seen. Immature birds are much browner and have a heavily spotted belly and dark underwing. Usually solitary, the Lanner sometimes flies in family groups, when adults teach young birds the skills they require.

Eurasian Hobby 36 cm | 14"

A very fast falcon with barred underparts and orange-red thighs. This migrant from Europe and Asia arrives in East Africa in September and always seems to be on the move. It is thought that most Eurasian Hobbies head as far south as South Africa before making the return journey, similar to the route taken by many Eurasian Bee-eaters (*page 151*).

Often found near water, this bird specializes in catching its prey on the wing, including swallows, martins and dragonflies. Needless to say, a capture happens very quickly and you have to be very lucky to observe it! Immature birds are browner than the grey-backed adults and lack the orange-red thighs. Its flight profile is reminiscent of a huge swift, with relatively long, narrow wings compared with Common Kestrel or Lanner Falcon.

Eurasian Hobby

Lanner Falcon

Common Kestrel

☐ **Common Kestrel** 33 cm | 13"
A brown-backed falcon with a long tail. Found in singles and groups, these kestrels are frequently seen hovering over the grass in search of small prey before diving steeply onto their quarry. The sexes are fairly similar although males show more grey in the head and tail; young birds are mostly brown. In flight, all birds show a dark band at the end of the tail. Resident birds, sometimes known as 'Rock Kestrels', are supplemented by migratory birds from Europe and Asia between October and April. Birds often come together to roost on the top of an acacia or desert palm tree, when you may hear their excited high-pitched calls "*kee-kee-kee*".

Male

Female

☐ Ostrich   250 cm | 98"

Huge, unmistakable birds. Males are distinguished by their black body feathers, white wing plumes and short, white tail. The pink skin of the head, neck and long, strong legs becomes flushed when birds are excited. This is particularly so during display, which involves exuberant rolling and shaking of the wing plumes. Females (*see page 256*) and immature birds are greyish-brown in colour and lack pink tones to the skin. Eggs are laid in a scrape in the ground that several females may share. The call is a deep "*hoo-hoo-whoooooo*" that sounds similar to a Lion's roar from a distance.

RECORD BREAKER - This is the largest bird in the world, lays the largest and heaviest eggs, and is the only flightless bird of mainland Africa. Although it is the only bird in the world with two toes on each foot, the Ostrich is capable of sprints in excess of 60 kph, making it the fastest-running of all birds.

☐ Southern Ground Hornbill

102 cm | 40"

Huge, black, turkey-like terrestrial birds of open and wooded grasslands. Usually encountered in family groups that may include immature birds and mature offspring of previous broods. Adults of both sexes show red facial skin and a saggy wattle, but the female can be separated by the small patch of violet-blue colour on the throat. Look out for the incredibly long eyelashes on this bird. They are reluctant fliers and prefer to hop and run away from danger but they will always fly to roost in trees at dusk when they reveal clean white outer flight feathers. Listen out for their wonderful calls, usually at dawn, a deep, booming "*ooomp-ooomp-wa-woomp*" that carries for many kilometres. Nowadays, this bird is most frequently seen within Lake Nakuru National Park and is rare elsewhere.

Female

These hornbills can walk for over 30 km a day in search of invertebrates, reptiles and young birds.

Juvenile

Female

111

Bustard and gamebirds

Male

Female

☐ **Black-bellied Bustard** 64 cm | 25" ▲
A small bustard of grassy plains. During the
breeding season (March to May), males perform
an amazing display, usually from raised ground
such as a grassy knoll. They stand with their
neck raised then throw back their head abruptly
making a "*kwaark*" sound. With the neck
coiled back, the bird then growls softly before
letting out the air in a belched "*pop!*" about five
seconds after the initial recoil. On a quiet day, it
is possible to hear other males making the same
display call just a short distance away. Adult birds
look spectacular in flight and show a strongly
contrasting black-and-white wing pattern which
is obvious from many kilometres away, especially
as the males make exaggerated wing flaps during
aerial circuits of their territories.

☐ **Helmeted Guineafowl** ▶
61 cm | 24"
A large, gregarious gamebird
with finely spotted plumage.
Despite its bare blue-and-
red skinned face and bony
helmet, this is an attractive
bird that feeds in the open but
needs trees nearby in which
to roost and take refuge from
its many predators. It is a
favourite with small cats, such
as Serval, and stealthy birds of
prey. The chicks exhibit rapid
wing growth and are able to
fly from danger when they are
just one week old.

■ Yellow-necked Spurfowl
40 cm | 16"

A scruffy brown fowl with a patch of bare yellow skin on the neck. Favouring dry areas in the southern Rift, this gamebird is not uncommon but can be difficult to find even though it lives in open areas. This is partly because it feeds in a crouched position, with the brightly coloured head well-hidden, and the back is well-camouflaged. It has large clutches of eggs and pairs may be seen with as many as 12 chicks at a time. However, they are heavily predated and entire broods can be lost. Compare this bird of open areas with the gamebirds of wooded areas, on *pages 132–133*.

▶

Across East Africa, the Kiswahili name for Helmeted Guineafowl is Kanga, a name that is also given to the colourful patterned cloth often worn by women as a skirt.

Temminck's Courser 21 cm | 8¼"

Small, erect-standing birds of the short grass plains. Usually found in pairs or small parties in very open areas, where they habitually run, stop and then peck at an item on the ground – often a small grub or other invertebrate. It is quite common to find them rummaging through a small dung pile, where various food items can be found. They are reluctant to fly, preferring to run from any threat, but when they do take flight they show a short tail, beyond which the long legs project, and very rounded wings that are entirely black underneath. This creates quite a distinctive silhouette.

☐ Heuglin's Courser ▶
27 cm | 10½"

A remarkably camouflaged nocturnal wader of dry areas. Although it probably occurs throughout much of the Rift Valley, this bird is notoriously difficult to find and is only recorded with regularity around Baringo, where the top local bird guides know exactly where to find it. Its plumage is not only an effective camouflage but also incredibly beautiful and any encounter with this bird should be savoured. When termites begin to emerge from their hills in vast numbers, these waders will break their nocturnal habits to feast on them in the daytime.

■ Black-headed Plover 25 cm | 10" ▲

A striking, upright wader of the dry north. Like most other dry-country waders, this comical-looking species is predominantly feeds at night, spending most of the daylight hours seeking shade under trees and bushes. Unlike many other waders of this habitat, this plover is not well-camouflaged and instead relies on good community relations. It is a gregarious species that looks out for its neighbours and will use mobbing tactics to deter predators from itself and its eggs, much like the Crowned Plover (*page 72*).

◄ ☐ Red-capped Lark
15 cm | 6"

An attractive small lark with a preference for short grass plains. The rich-rufous cap and chest patches on this bird contrast with the otherwise plain plumage, making it easily separable from the streaky-breasted Rufous-naped Lark. Young birds are greyish and heavily peppered with pale feather edges. In flight, the tail appears very dark but shows lighter brown outer tail feathers. The simple call comprises a series of dry "*chirrp*" notes.

◄ ☐ Pink-breasted Lark
16 cm | 6½"

A distinctive lark of dry scrub. Often heard well before it is seen, this rather dull species can appear more like a pipit (slim) than a lark (chunky) but a good view shows the warm cinnamon-orange tones (it is not really pink!) to the face, breast and flanks. It sings a descending ramble loudly from an exposed perch, such as a treetop or power line, before dropping to the ground with a parachuting descent.

Habitat preference plays an important part in identifying similar species like larks.

Rather strangely, and despite the bird's name, the rufous nape – the feathers between the crown and the neck – is rarely seen.

Rufous-naped Lark 18 cm | 7"

The common, chunky, brown-streaked lark of long grass plains. This drab-looking bird is frequently encountered on drives through the grassy plains when it springs up from tracks and verges, displaying an obvious chestnut wing patch. Sometimes, birds will run in front of vehicles and avoid taking flight. If you observe this, look out for the obvious crest. The song of this bird is the quintessential sound of the grassy plains, a pleasant whistled "*see-seeuu*" which translates usefully to "*hey Joey*". The similar Crested and Red-winged Larks do not occur in the region covered in this guide.

Display

Male

Female

Grassland Pipit 17 cm | 6½"

A common streaky-backed bird of open areas. Pipits are unobtrusive brown birds that walk with a strut, quite like the more gaudy wagtails (*page 80*) to which they are closely related. Several similar species of pipit occur in the Rift Valley but this is the most abundant and frequently seen. It is also closely related to the Yellow-throated Longclaw but easily separated from that species by the lack of yellow tones in its plumage. In flight, Grassland Pipit shows very white outer tail feathers – a useful identification feature when considering other similar species.

Fischer's Sparrow Lark 11 cm | 4½"

A tiny lark with a distinctive face pattern. This charming little lark can be encountered in open grassland where it often feeds very close to tracks and roads. It has a tendency to fly off at the last minute, usually when you have not even seen it well, but if you are driving slowly it may fly just a short distance before dropping down again. The males have obvious white cheeks set in a dark head, the crown and neck being chestnut in colour. Females and immatures lack the dark head but show some chestnut markings on the neck and above the eyes. The soft-grey back colour separates this bird from the darker Chestnut-backed Sparrow Lark (*not shown*), which is more common east of the Rift.

Yellow-throated Longclaw
22 cm | 8¾"

A yellow-breasted, terrestrial bird with a preference for long grass plains. Males are easily identified by their bright plumage while females and immatures are much more streaky with duller yellow features. Birds are often seen along tracks and are easily flushed into the air when they glide on sharply flicked, flat wings and reveal two white squares on the end of the tail. They can be difficult to follow in the grass when they have their brown, streaked backs towards you. The high-pitched call "*wi-pi-pi-pi*" is frequently heard in flight. Compare with the rare Sharpe's Longclaw featured on *page 19*.

Longclaws get their name from the very long claw at the back of the foot.

Capped Wheatear   17 cm | 6¾"

An attractive chat of short grass plains. With its distinctive face pattern and upright stance, the Capped Wheatear is difficult to confuse with any of the other resident birds. It is found singly or in pairs in areas of open, short grass with scattered rocks, sometimes close to small villages. It routinely bobs and pumps its tail. In flight, birds show an obvious white rump that contrasts with an all-black tail, a distinctive pattern that easily separates this species from the migratory wheatears on *pages 122–123*.

▼

Northern Anteater Chat

18 cm | 7"

A common dark-brown chat of open areas that shows a large white flash in the flight feathers. Usually encountered in extended family groups, these chocolate-brown chats prefer open areas with good vantage points, such as boulders and fence-posts. Here, territorial males will frequently burst into song, holding their wings down and raising the tail in excitement. The sexes are similar.

▶

The family name 'wheatear' has nothing to do with 'wheat' or 'ears' but is an old English corruption of 'white-arse' on account of the conspicuous white rump.

☐ Abyssinian Wheatear 15 cm | 6"

A dark chat of rocky ground with a pale crown and reddish rump and tail. With its preference for grassy and rocky hillsides, this dark-backed wheatear is common in the Rift Valley where conditions are suitable but is not found elsewhere in Kenya. It is the only wheatear in the region that shows a reddish rather than a white rump. Females are pale brown and do not have a contrasting crown, while juvenile birds are black all-over apart from a white belly. This species is also widely known as Schalow's Wheatear.

▼

Male

Female

Male

Female

☐ **Northern Wheatear** 15cm | 6" ▲

A common migrant chat with an obvious
white rump. This pale wheatear could be
encountered between September and April
almost anywhere but shows a preference for
open areas. Males in spring look very smart
with their grey and black plumage, while
females and immatures are mostly
buffy-brown. Both sexes of all ages are
eye-catching in flight when the white
rump flashes before you. Like other
migrant wheatears, it is mostly silent
in the region. This incredible bird is
among the smallest of the long-distance
migrants to reach East Africa and
many individuals breed well
inside the Arctic Circle.

Male

Pied Wheatear 15 cm | 6"

This is a rather dark migrant wheatear with a white rump, which arrives into the Rift from its breeding grounds in Asia and eastern Europe in September and departs by April. Males are very distinctive birds with a black face, throat and back but are otherwise very pale. They resemble the Abyssinian Wheatear (*page 121*) but have a white rather than a reddish rump. Females are similar to female Northern Wheatear but are darker brown on the breast and back. These wheatears habitually fly into trees when disturbed and are typically found in more scrubby areas than the Northern Wheatear.

Male

Female

Whinchat 13 cm | 5"

A small migrant chat with a conspicuous eyebrow and streaky back. This delicate little bird can be told from similar chats and wheatears by its dark-brown cheeks, orange-buff breast, pale stripe over the eye and black tail with white at the base. It is fairly common during the northern winter and is particularly fond of grassy areas with prominent perches, such as fence posts, from which it drops onto its insect prey. The 'whin' in the name is an old English reference to a thorny shrub, such as gorse.

Crows are capable of complex problem-solving and one of the few bird families that have a proven ability to count.

☐ **Cape Rook** 43 cm | 17" ▲

An all-black crow with a slim bill, also known as the Black Crow. Like the Pied Crow, this species is very much at home in the company of people and is common along the main roads and villages though the Rift Valley, but is less common north of Nakuru. It is not as bulky as the other crow species shown here, usually appears long-legged on the ground and looks slimmer in flight due to its narrow wings and long, slender tail.

Pied Crow 46 cm | 18"

A large, black bird with a white breast and neck. Like many other crows around the world, this is a clever opportunist that forages around towns and villages in search of food. It will often steal food from other birds and animals, and may then store the bounty for leaner times. The gruff "*caar-caar*" notes are typically crow-like. The largest crow in the region is the White-naped Raven (*not shown*) that may sometimes be found in the higher parts of the Rift Valley but that bird shows a very thick bill and a black breast.

Fan-tailed Raven 46 cm | 18"

An all-black crow with a short, heavy bill. The Fan-tailed Raven shows a very distinctive silhouette in flight, the short tail and very broad wings merging to create an almost tail-less form. When on the ground, it is less upright and appears shorter-legged than the Cape Rook. It is only likely to be encountered near cliffs in the northern part of the Rift Valley, in the vicinity of Lakes Baringo and Bogoria.

Pied Crow

Fan-tailed Raven

As with all widowbirds, the males of these beautiful species acquire their elegant breeding colours and long tail feathers at the onset of the first rains (usually the end of October), in readiness for the breeding season. After the second rains and at the end of the breeding season (around June) the males lose their striking plumage and look very similar to the females of the species.

☐ Long-tailed Widowbird
breeding male 72 cm | 28";
female 15 cm | 6"

An unmistakable black songbird with an extremely long, tapering tail. The glossy-black breeding males have a bright red shoulder-patch that is emphasized by a cream border. This feature is retained during the non-breeding season when males otherwise look similar to the brown and streaky females. Although non-breeding birds wander widely in mixed flocks, breeding birds are fairly easy to find on the eastern slopes of the Rift, especially on wet grasslands in the Kinangop area.

Male

Female

Males fly over their grassland territories with an exaggerated flapping flight.

Long-tailed Widowbird

Red-collared Widowbird

Widowbirds are named after their black 'lady-in-mourning' plumage.

☐ Red-collared Widowbird
breeding male 25 cm | 10":
female 12·5 cm | 5"

An attractive black songbird with a long, wispy tail. Males in breeding dress show a red crown that extends down the sides of the face to form a red collar. In the territorial flight, each of the long and scruffy tail feathers dangle independently. Like other widowbird species, the Red-collared Widowbird is polygamous (*i.e.* males will mate with several females within their territory). Females are similar to other female widowbirds and bishops but typically show a yellow stripe over the eye and have a yellow wash across the unstreaked breast.

Male

Female

Jackson's Widowbird breeding male 30 cm | 12"; female 14 cm | 5½"

Dark birds of long grass plains with long, drooping tails. The Rift Valley is home to a very important population of this scarce and local bird that depends on large tracts of moist, open grassland. Breeding males are blackish with brown 'shoulder' patches and a sickle-shaped tail. Look out for displaying birds between February and June (during the second rains), when they fly up from the long grass before parachuting down again. Females and non-breeding males are brown and stripy and incredibly difficult to separate from other female and non-breeding male widowbirds and bishops. Flocks are often seen flying, squadron-like, low over grassland.

Named after Sir Frederick Jackson (1859–1929), an English administrator, explorer and ornithologist who became the first Governor of Kenya.

Male

Female

▪ Northern Red Bishop 11 cm | 4½"

Brilliant red-and-black weaver of the northern lakes. Although not common throughout
the Rift Valley, it is an enigmatic species that many consider a 'must-see'. It is easiest
to find from January to June around lakes Baringo and Bogoria, when males call and
display from prominent perches in wet grassland and marshes. Females are similar to
other bishops and widowbirds but smaller. The Southern Red Bishop (*not shown*) is very
similar and may be encountered at the other end of the Rift Valley, around Lake Magadi.

Bishops are named after the red robes of bishops, the plumage
of the males of many species in this group being red-and-black.
The Yellow Bishop is one of several exceptions.

▪ Yellow Bishop 15 cm | 6"

A bird of the grassland edge. Males have black
body plumage with a yellow 'shoulder' patch
and a bright yellow rump in all plumages.
They have an energetic display flight that involves
jumping from a perch and flapping rapidly before
dropping down with a soar. During this show,
males puff up their yellow rumps and call a rapid,
high-pitched "*tli-tli-tli-tli*". Females are brown and
streaked, like the other species shown here.

Male

Male

Northern Red Bishop

Non-breeding male

Female

Yellow Bishop

Female

129

☐ Winding Cisticola 13 cm | 5" ▶

A common, streaky brown warbler
of wet grasslands and marshes.
Of the many cisticolas to be found
in the Rift Valley, the Winding
Cisticola is among the easiest
to identify by sight. It shows
an unstreaked chestnut crown
(compare with Stout Cisticola),
a heavily streaked grey back and
very obvious chestnut wings
and tail. Its song is a distinctive
"reeling" sound that is quite
similar to that of Stout Cisticola.

At least 15 species of cisticola
have been recorded in Kenya's
Rift Valley and only a few show
distinctive colouration. They are
notoriously difficult to identify by
sight and are best separated by
habitat preference and their
unique calls, many of which are
included in their common names,
as is the case with Winding
Cisticola. Don't be too hard on
yourself if they all look the same
– but do concentrate on learning
first the ones that you see and
hear most often.

African Quailfinch   9 cm | 3½"   ▲

An attractive but shy finch of open grasslands. Often first seen when flushed from the edge of tracks, African Quailfinch utter a high-pitched "*chink chink-chink*" call as they fly off, usually just a short distance before dropping down again. Males are more boldly marked than females. Like many other seed-eating birds, this finch requires regular access to water and therefore tends to favour moist grasslands. It can survive relatively dry spells as long as puddles persist but birds will wander widely in search of water.

Stout Cisticola   13 cm | 5"

A streaky grey-brown warbler of open grasslands. Unlike the Winding Cisticola, this warbler is less fond of marshes and is more at home on big open grasslands, such as those on the Soysambu Estate. It can easily be identified by its streaked chestnut crown that contrasts with an unstreaked chestnut nape, heavily streaked grey-brown back and lack of any chestnut colouration in the wings. It also shows a blackish tail when flying away, unlike Winding Cisticola which has a chestnut tail. The reeling song of this bird starts with a few abrupt notes spitted out before breaking into a reeling trill that is otherwise similar to Winding Cisticola.

Desert Cisticola"   10 cm | 4"

A very small and streaky-backed cisticola of short, dry grass and low thorny scrub. It is best identified by its preference for very short grass; the other two cisticolas shown here prefer longer and more lush grass. The Desert Cisticola is common in the Rift Valley floor from Lake Magadi in the south to Lake Elementeita in the north. Its plumage usually appears greyish and 'cold' (*i.e.* it mostly lacks the warm brown tones of many other cisticolas), although it does show an unstreaked pale-rufous rump. Its call is a monotonous "*p-jink-p-jink-p-jink*", which is often given in flight and accompanied by the snapping of its wings.

☐ Scaly Francolin
31 cm | 12¼"

A plain-looking francolin with a red bill and red legs. At first glance this retiring gamebird often appears just grey and not particularly scaly but, given a good view, the delicate pattern is there to see. It prefers to keep to bushy cover but it is quite tame if stumbled upon when on foot. It is less vocal than the Red-necked Spurfowl and you are more likely to hear its soft, purring "*kwoorr*" contact call than the louder "*ker-RAK-ker RAK*" territorial call.

An average clutch is six eggs and these francolins have an unusual habit of incubating by night and deserting by day, perhaps to keep predators off the scent.

☐ Crested Francolin
30 cm | 12"

A stripy, bantam-like gamebird. This drab francolin has a preference for dry, open bush where it often gathers in large family groups. The sexes look similar, although females show more barring on the upperparts than males, especially on the rump. The short crest, after which the bird is named, can be difficult to see unless birds are excited, but look out for the cocked tail that is usually raised.

The Scaly Francolin is more likely to be encountered in woodland at higher altitudes than the other species shown here.

Hildebrandt's Francolin 41 cm | 16"

A large, shy francolin of dense cover.
You will almost certainly hear this francolin before you see it – and heaven forbid that you are trying to nap when it gets going! The shrieking territorial call "*kik-kerik-kerik-kerik*" gets louder and louder and then, if you're really unlucky, the female joins in. These are the largest francolins in the Kenyan Rift and appear more round than others. Males are heavily spotted with black on the front and neck, while females are rich-brown on the belly.

This bird was named in honour of Johann Maria Hildebrandt (1847–1881), a German collector who travelled extensively to East Africa, Madagascar and the Comoro Islands.

General note: The names spurfowl and francolin are often used interchangeably for the same species, the actual difference being minimal. In East Africa, the name spurfowl is given to those species that show bare throat skin, and francolin to those that do not. The South Africans take a different stance, with Scaly and Hildebrandt's Francolins being called Spurfowl. It's a funny old 'game'!

Male

Female

☐ Laughing Dove 23 cm | 9"

A small, rufous-and-grey-winged dove. Common in drier areas, and often on open ground, this species still requires trees in which to nest and is rarely found far from cover. It lacks the black neck collar of the other doves shown here but has a black-and-rusty mottled patch high on the chest. In flight, it appears slender and shows large white corners to the long, dark-centred tail that are more obvious than those of Ring-necked Dove. It has a wide distribution, being found from south-western Europe, where it is also known as the Palm Dove, eastwards across much of Asia and most of Africa. Its call is a gentle giggling *"hoo-woo-woo-woo-woo"*, hence the bird's name.

▼

▲ ■ African Olive Pigeon
38 cm | 15"
A dark forest pigeon with yellow legs. Common in the well-wooded areas of Lake Nakuru National Park, though less so elsewhere, this attractive pigeon sometimes forms sizeable flocks around fruiting trees but is otherwise fairly solitary. When seen from below, the white spotting on the belly is a diagnostic identificaton feature. In flight, it lacks any white or grey in the tail and rump. Males are told by their bright-yellow bill.

◀ ■ Speckled Pigeon
34 cm | 13½"
A large, heavily spotted pigeon, common in and around towns and villages. The brown wings are peppered with white spots and in flight the rump shows as pale-grey and the tail is bordered with black. The grey head contrasts with a patch of bare red skin around the eyes and the chest is delicately streaked with maroon. Just like urban pigeons, this bird has a habit of clapping its wings on take-off.

'Collared' doves

☐ Ring-necked Dove 25 cm | 10"

A common beige-coloured dove of gardens and lightly wooded areas. The black collar at the back of the neck, after which this bird is named, is also shared with the other species on this page. In flight, the upperwing shows a pale-grey stripe that contrasts with the darker flight feathers, and the light-brown tail has white triangles at each corner which is a useful aid when the bird flies away. The well-loved call is one of the easiest of all to remember, a softly purred "*pur-PUR-pur*", commonly translated to "work harder" (mornings) or "more lager" (evenings)! It is known as the Cape Turtle Dove across southern Africa.

◄ ☐ Red-eyed Dove 32 cm | 12½"

A large, dark-brown dove with a black collar and a bright rosy flush. Showing more of a preference for well-wooded areas than the Ring-necked Dove, the Red-eyed Dove is a dark grey-brown on the back, has grey on the belly and, in flight, shows a smoky-grey tail with a broad blackish band across the middle. Although the red eye and eye-ring can be difficult to see, the pink flush to the neck and breast is obvious and contrasts with the white forehead. Its call is a bouncy series of purred notes that usefully translates to "*I am a Red-eyed Dove*", often repeated over and over.

◄ ☐ African Mourning Dove 30 cm | 12"

The common beige-coloured dove at Lake Baringo. This dove is usually associated with water so it is perhaps surprising that with so many lakes within the Rift Valley, it is only found at one. It is very similar to the widespread Ring-necked Dove but shows blue tones on the head and a white iris that is edged with bright-red skin. In addition to a number of coo-ing notes, this bird has a fantastic call that is unforgettable once heard, a downward purring "*AAA-ooooowww*".

Collared Doves of the Rift Valley

These three species may appear very similar at first but once you 'get your eye in' they can easily be separated. Among the best features to check on any birds seen are the general colour tone (Red-eyed appears darker than the others with a rosy flush to the plumage), eye colour (both Red-eyed and Ring-necked Doves appear dark but Mourning Dove is obviously pale with conspicuous red rings around the eyes), and overall size (Red-eyed is largest and Ring-necked is smallest). In flight, only Red-eyed Dove lacks an obvious white tip to the tail. Finally, habitat preference can also be very useful. If you spend just a few minutes getting familiar with the birds you see well, you will be identifying these species like an expert in no time!

Female

Male

Namaqua Dove" ▲
25 cm | 10"

A small, slim dove of dry country with a long, pointed tail. The sexes are similar in shape but males show a distinctive black face, throat and breast. Like the Blue-spotted Wood Dove, males also show a reddish bill with a yellow tip and glossy, bluish-purple wing spots. Young birds appear very scaly. This dove has a fast and direct flight, when it shows chestnut-brown in the flight feathers.

Blue-spotted Wood Dove ▶
20 cm | 8"

An uncommon dove with a yellow-tipped bill. With a preference for thick woodland and forest, this species is only reliably found at Lake Nakuru National Park, where it can often be seen alongside the various tracks. It is very similar in appearance to the Emerald-spotted Wood Dove but the reddish bill with a yellow tip is diagnostic. It often looks more uniform brown on the wings than the Emerald-spotted Wood Dove, and the number of glossy wing spots is typically fewer. Its call is very similar to that of the Emerald-spotted Wood Dove but does not last as long.

Emerald-spotted Wood Dove" ▼

20 cm | 8"

A small, colourful dove of dry, wooded areas, usually seen running around on the woodland floor with an action similar to a clockwork toy. If disturbed, it shoots into the air with a rapid burst of wing-beats, showing chestnut flight feathers and a grey rump and tail with narrow black bars. The frequently heard call is a series of muffled "coo" notes that start with a rise (exactly like the first four notes of *Rule Britannia* for those who know it) before simultaneously falling in tone and speeding up, finishing on a rapid, pulsating flourish. This will make sense when you hear it! The glossy emerald wing-spots may appear black or shiny-blue in some lights, but be careful not to confuse this common bird with the Blue-spotted Wood Dove that shows a dark-red bill with a yellow tip.

■ African Green Pigeon   27 cm | 10½" ▼

A spectacular bright-green pigeon. Usually found feeding in the top of fruiting trees, especially fig, these gorgeous lime-green birds have a peculiar call that is quite unlike that of other pigeons and doves. It starts with a soft "*hoo-hoo-wee-oo*" followed by excited whinnying and a few yelped "*whip-hoo-woo-whip*" notes before ending softly with "*ku-KU-ku-ku*". If you are lucky enough to see it well, look out for the red bill with a white tip, red legs and lilac shoulder-patch. As they depend on emerging fruits, birds will commute great distances from their roosting sites to visit favoured fruiting trees.

The infamously extinct Dodo of Mauritius in the Indian Ocean was a giant flightless pigeon, closely related to the green pigeons, which became island-bound as the commuting distance between island and mainland became too great over millions of years.

Meyer's Parrot 23 cm | 9" ▶

A medium-sized, brown parrot with a green belly and splashes of yellow, often seen in pairs and small family groups. Meyer's Parrot is also known as Brown Parrot, which seems a shame as it carries so many other bright colours. The noisy screeches, given in flight and when perched, mean that you are unlikely to miss it if it is around. Young birds lack the yellow on the crown but are otherwise similar to adults. It is found where fruiting trees, especially the Kenya Greenheart, occur.

Named after Dr Bernhard Meyer (1767–1836) who was a physician by profession but a keen ornithologist in his spare time. Oddly, it is thought he never actually travelled to Africa where this species is found.

Hybrid lovebird 15 cm | 6" ▶

A charming and colourful small parrot. This free-flying hybrid is the result of cross-breeding between two introduced species, the Yellow-collared and Fischer's Lovebirds, both of which are native to northern Tanzania. Pure Fischer's Lovebirds show an orange head and Yellow-collared Lovebirds show a black head, but most of the Rift Valley hybrids show a blotched pattern. They gather in sizeable flocks to feed and roost, and tend to nest in tree holes. Although they may not belong here, they are surely a welcome and colourful addition to many gardens in the area.

■ White-bellied Go-away-bird 50 cm | 20"

A large, grey bird with a tall crest and long tail. Often seen in pairs or groups, this go-away-bird does not scream "*Go Away*" like its southern African relative the Grey Go-away-bird (*not shown*). Instead it calls "*WAH*" very loudly and runs along the branches of trees in great excitement, often hopping from one to the next. The white belly is obvious when the underside is seen and in flight the bird shows distinctive white bands across the dark wings and tail. It is a close relative of the brightly coloured turacos but lacks their colourful plumage.

Often called the 'water-bottle bird' because of its distinctive call, a rapid series of bubbling "*woo-woo-woo-woo*" notes that fall before rising with a stammer at the end.

Immature birds, often seen being fed by their smaller foster parents, such as this White-browed Robin Chat, are dark grey-brown above with a white, strongly barred belly.

Juvenile

▢ Red-chested Cuckoo ▶

30 cm | 12"

A hawk-like bird with barred underparts. Often referred to as the 'Rain-bird', these elusive cuckoos are a common feature of the wooded highlands of East Africa on account of their loud, three-note call "*wip-wip-weeu*", which translates to "*it will rain*". Professional meteorologists have nothing to fear, however, as these birds call during the well-known rainy seasons – and quite frequently after the rain has already started! Adults are dark-grey across the upperparts, show a pale-grey head, and have a rich-chestnut band across the chest. Like most African cuckoos, they are brood-parasites, laying their eggs in the active nests of other species, particularly the robin chat species on *pages 174–175*.

Adult

◀ ▢ White-browed Coucal   41 cm | 16"

A bulky brown bird of wet and lightly bushed areas. Closely related to the cuckoos, coucals raise their own young and make grassy, domed nests in tall grass or thick vegetation. They are weak fliers and rarely wander far from the centre of their territory. Coucals appear rather ungainly on the ground but spend much of their time walking stealthily through vegetation in search of a meal – this can include eggs, baby birds, reptiles and amphibians.

A male is shown; female and immature birds are much browner on the back with heavily barred underparts.

Male

Male

Female

▲ ☐ **Klaas's Cuckoo** 18 cm | 7"

An emerald-green cuckoo of woodland and gardens. About the size of a Common Bulbul (*page 170*), this small cuckoo is a brood-parasite of sunbirds, favouring the Collared Sunbird (*page 207*). Males are iridescent green on the head and black-and-white on the front, whilst females are browner and heavily barred. Both sexes show a fleck of white behind the eye. In flight, they reveal white outer tail feathers so could be confused with a honeyguide (*pages 164–165*), which shows the same feature. The call is unmistakable, a whistled two-note "*phwee-phuu*", the second note lower than the first, which is often repeated three times.

Named after the Khoi Khoi servant of French explorer and collector Francois Le Vaillant (1753–1824) who presumably found the bird for him. Le Vaillant also named the Bateleur (*page 104*).

Diederik Cuckoo 19 cm | 7½"

A heavily barred cuckoo with a distinctive call.
This bird can be found in a variety of habitats,
from open woodland to dry acacia scrub. During
the wet season, from October to June, you are
likely to find it close to the communal hanging
nests of several weaver species (particularly
those on *page 219*), where the female cuckoo
lays her eggs while the weavers are not at home.
Superficially similar to the Klaas's Cuckoo, the
Diederik Cuckoo is a slightly larger bird with
many white spots on the wing and barring on the
underparts, including the underwing in flight.
The bird's name derives from its loud call, a
resonant "*dee-dee-DEE-der-ick*".

Green Wood-hoopoe 37 cm | 14½" ▶

A gregarious glossy-black bird
with a long tail. Often encountered
in family groups among the
Yellow-barked Acacia trees
that surround the Rift Valley
lakes, the Green Wood-hoopoe
appears black on first impression,
but good light will reveal an
iridescent gloss to the plumage,
mostly violet on the wings and tail
but green on the head and back.
The strong, pointed, red bill is
slightly curved and is used to probe
tree bark on boughs and trunks for
invertebrates. The feet are red and
its long tail is dark with white
spots along the outer edge. In
flight, the wings show a broad
white bar across the flight
feathers and a single white
spot at the front. They
appear quite clumsy
as they fly from tree
to tree, and stay
in contact with
chuckling calls.

Some ornithologists split the Hoopoe into two species – African Hoopoe and Eurasian Hoopoe. The differences are clear to the trained eye but are beyond the scope of this guide.

Hoopoe 28 cm | 11"

A bright-orange bird with black-and-white stripes in the wing. Unmistakable, with an erectile crest, the Hoopoe can vary in colour from orange to light peachy-brown according to the time of year. It feeds on the ground with a stitching motion, probing the ground with its decurved bill for grubs and worms. On take-off, it shows an elaborate pied decoration of stripes through the rounded wings and tail. It prefers to nest in tree holes but will also use holes in stone walls or sandy banks. The call is a low, two- or three-note series "*poop-poop-poop*".

▼

☐ Blue-naped Mousebird
35 cm | 14"

A small grey bird with a long tail. Similar in size and shape to the Speckled Mousebird, the Blue-naped Mousebird prefers much drier, open habitats and is particularly fond of acacia. Its plumage is mostly grey, rather than brown as in Speckled Mousebird, the cheeks are plain (rather than white), and it has a red eye-patch extending to the base of the bill. It also shows a more pronounced, stiff crest which adds to its elegant appearance. Listen out for the distinctive high-pitched "*peeu-peeu-peeu*" call when in flight, which is rapid and direct rather than clumsy and weak as in Speckled Mousebird.

Formerly known as Coly-birds (the scientific genus remains *Colius*), these cute balls of feather were once given as gifts between the Lords, Ladies and gentry of the day. It is thought that the 'Four Calling Birds' alluded to in the *12 Days of Christmas* carol is a corruption from the original 'Four Coly-birds', but this changed over time because nobody knew what a Coly-bird was.

☐ **Speckled Mousebird** 33 cm | 13"

A small-bodied brown bird with a long, stiff tail. This comical little bird is often seen clambering through bushes and thick vegetation when it really does appear quite mouse-like and where it feeds on seeds and fruit. Like the Blue-naped Mousebird, it is a gregarious species but the combination of white cheeks and black throat is a useful identification feature. Good views will also reveal pale cheeks and pink feet. The call is a simple chattering *"chir-chir-chir-chir-chir"* that drops in tone.

◀

Striped Kingfisher 17 cm | 6¾"

An unobtrusive and rather dowdy kingfisher. This bird is often found far from water, where it is a specialist hunter of grasshoppers and other sizeable invertebrates. The bill is dark above and red below – the reverse of Woodland Kingfisher – and it shows a dark mask through the eye. Like the Grey-headed Kingfisher, its blue colouration is restricted to the wings and tail. Although shy and sometimes difficult to find, the Striped Kingfisher becomes extravert during its display, when it lands on an exposed perch, opens it wings, and calls a long, pulsating "*wi-frreeeeewww*".

Woodland Kingfisher
22 cm | 8¾"

A brilliant sky-blue kingfisher with a red-and-black bill. With its bright colours, dazzling display and unforgettable call, this bird is a favourite among guides and safari-goers alike. Usually found in lightly wooded areas, the Woodland Kingfisher is the bluest of the bush kingfishers and shows a bright red upper half to the bill and black lower half. Like the Striped Kingfisher, it displays with open blue wings, and calls a penetrating "*CHEW-chhrreerrrr*". It will happily feed on small lizards and amphibians, as well as invertebrates.

General note: These kingfishers are not restricted to water and feed primarily on invertebrates rather than fish. The colour of the bill, face and back are all useful identification features and the calls are distinctive. Their scientific genus *Halcyon* stems from the mythical Alcyon bird, which produced 14 days of calm weather during the northern winter. Hence, today, Halcyon days are calm and cloud-free.

■ Grey-headed Kingfisher ▶
21 cm | 8¼"

A dark-backed kingfisher with a pale head. Often found in bush and lightly wooded areas, sometimes close to water, this kingfisher shows a grey head and breast and a chestnut belly, whilst the wing-tips and tail are bright blue – most obvious when seen in flight. Its bill is all-red, although young birds may show a dark tip. It is less vocal than the other kingfishers shown here but you may still hear the softly chipped "*tit-tit-tit-tit*" notes that comprise its call.

Eurasian
Bee-eater

☐ Eurasian Bee-eater 28 cm | 11"

A stunning migrant from Europe that is often
seen migrating overhead in sizeable flocks.
Birds typically appear on their southward journey
between the end of September and early November,
and then again heading north in March and April,
although small numbers are suspected to spend
their winter in southern Kenya. Listen for their soft,
churring "*prruut-prruut*" calls as they drift leisurely
overhead, and enjoy watching them make dashing
flights after bees, wasps and dragonflies.

☐ Blue-cheeked Bee-eater 30 cm | 12"

A brilliant-green bee-eater with a long, pointed tail.
Often seen perched in open bush, and frequently near
water, this stunner shows a rich rufous colouration to
the underwing in flight. It is a migrant from the Near
East, arriving in October and departing around April,
while the similar Madagascar Bee-eater (*not shown*),
which sports a rusty-brown cap and has less blue in the
face, visits the region from May to September. The calls
of both species are a series of trilled "*preep*" notes.

Blue-cheeked
Bee-eater

☐ White-throated Bee-eater 28 cm | 11"

A colourful bee-eater with a black collar and cap.
As the name suggests, this beauty shows an obvious
white throat in all plumages but only the adults have
the long central tail-streamers. During any encounter
with this bird, look out for the kaleidoscope of colours
and its long bill. It breeds in small numbers around
Lake Magadi but most birds seen in the region will be
migrants from dry areas of Africa south of the Sahara.

White-throated
Bee-eater

These three species are among the most stunning birds to grace the skies of the Serengeti
and NCA but, sadly, none of them are resident in the area covered in this guide. As explained
in their species accounts above, they are all migrants from further afield. The White-throated
Bee-eater breeds in the lower Rift Valley, just 100 km north-east of the Ngorongoro Crater, but
remains an irregular visitor throughout the year with a peak in observations occurring between
December and May. The other two species are longer-distance migrants and are only likely to
be encountered between September and April. Because of their wandering habits, all three
are mostly encountered in the air, where they take advantage of local insect populations with
amazing grace and agility. If you are fortunate enough to see any of these species perched,
perhaps resting during migration, take full advantage and consider it a very special sighting.

■ White-fronted Bee-eater 23 cm | 9" ▲

A green-backed bee-eater with a red and white chin. This large and brightly coloured bee-eater has a square tail and a brilliant blue vent. Like other resident species on this page, this bird shows a cinnamon-buff breast and belly but the face is brigher, with a red and white throat and a white forehead. It nests in high sand banks in the central Rift, particularly around Lakes Naivasha, Elementeita and Nakuru, sometimes in close proximity to the other species on this page.

▲ ■ Cinnamon-chested Bee-eater
22 cm | 8¾"
A green-backed bee-eater with a yellow throat and dark cinnamon underparts. This species is very similar to Little Bee-eater but larger, much darker below and lacks the narrow blue line above the black eye-mask of that species. Despite their physical similarities, habitat preference is probably the best way to separate the two, with this species requiring good stands of mature trees in well-wooded areas from where they dart after their airborne insect prey.

▲ ■ Little Bee-eater 15 cm | 6"
A colourful darting bird of open scrub. As the name suggests, these birds and most of the other species in this family specialize in a diet of bees, wasps and other insects that they catch in flight at breakneck speed. They are often found perched low down on the edge of bushes, where they wait for their prey to fly by, and call with a series of dry "*chip*" notes.

Little Bee-eaters typically nest in a burrow in a sandy bank that is often close to water although some very peculiar exceptions occur; the author has enjoyed watching a pair of these spritely little birds nesting in a pile of sand that had been dumped in a car park.

Rufous-crowned Roller 33 cm | 13"

A solid-looking roller lacking blue-green tones. This species is often found perched on overhead wires close to Lakes Baringo and Bogoria, and on first impression appears streaky and bull-headed. It may not be as bright as the other rollers but it is still a colourful bird with a purplish-pink head and breast. The strong, square-ended tail lacks streamers and is deep purplish-blue, the same colour as the flight feathers, and it lacks pale-blue patches in flight. This bird is known as the Purple Roller in southern Africa.

▼

Lilac-breasted Roller 38 cm | 15"

A spectacular roller that is a kaleidoscope of colours. Among the most popular of all birds on a safari circuit, this crow-sized jewel can be found across a variety of habitats in the Rift and is often located on a prominent tree branch over grassland from which it drops onto its favoured prey of beetles, grasshoppers and other invertebrates. In flight, it reveals brilliant-blue feathers in the wings. These rollers nest in tree holes and are very territorial, chasing mammals and other birds, including huge eagles, away from the nest area. This is when you are most likely to hear their throaty "*kerr-kerr-kerr*" call. Adults are easily told from the migrant Eurasian Roller by the long streamers at the sides of the tail, although these are lacking in the duller immature birds.

▼

Rollers are so named because of their exuberant 'rolling' display flights.

Lilac-breasted Roller

Eurasian Roller

☐ Eurasian Roller
31 cm | 12¼"

A colourful seasonal migrant to the region. At first glance this roller appears similar to the resident Lilac-breasted Roller but can quickly be separated by its all-blue head, throat and breast and, in flight, a richer chestnut 'saddle' on the back. The tail is also shorter and lacks the long tail streamers. The Eurasian Roller arrives from Europe during the October–November rains, when the plumage can appear 'washed out' or pale. After heading to southern Africa for several months it returns north again in March and April, when its colours are bright and fresh. Although vocal on their breeding grounds, they are generally silent on migration.

Female

Male

Female

Male

As with the species on *pages 158–159,* these medium-sized hornbills seal the entrance to their nest hole with mud to deter predators and nest-site rivals. The imprisoned female is wholly dependant upon the busy male that has to keep her well-fed through a small opening.

☐ Von der Decken's Hornbill
48 cm | 19"

A black-backed hornbill with a red or black bill of the southern Rift. These birds are slow-moving and rather clumsy inhabitants of acacia thicket, where they feed on a variety of fruits, invertebrates and small reptiles. Males show a bright-red bill with a yellow tip, while the bill of the females is black. Unlike the other hornbills shown here, Von der Decken's Hornbill has an unspotted back in both sexes and two large white wing-panels, most obvious during its undulating flight. Its call is a low, unassuming *"kuk-kuk-kuk-kuk".*

Named after Baron Carl Claus von der Decken (1833–1865), a German explorer who was the first European to attempt a Kilimanjaro summit climb. He failed.

☐ Jackson's Hornbill
48 cm | 19"

A spot-winged hornbill with a thick red or black bill of the northern Rift. Considered by some to be a subspecies of the Von der Decken's Hornbill, this bird is structurally very similar but easily identified by its heavily spotted wings. It is especially easy to find around Lake Baringo where it has become very tame at some lakeshore camps. Here it has also become a problem as it sometimes attacks vehicle mirrors and windscreen wipers.

See Jackson's Widowbird (*page 128*) to learn about Sir Frederick Jackson.

☐ Red-billed Hornbill 45 cm | 18"

A slender hornbill with spotted wings and a pale face. Unlike the other two species on this page, both sexes of this common dry-country hornbill show a red bill. The Red-billed Hornbill is more gregarious, especially in open areas, whereas the other two species shown here are generally encountered in pairs. Birds stay in contact with a long series of honked notes, and they may bow their heads while they do so.

▼

☐ Hemprich's Hornbill 60 cm | 24"

A large cliff-dwelling hornbill with a dull-red bill and dark eyes. Although this species is most frequently seen around Lake Baringo, and on the rocky islands within the lake, it has also been recorded as far south as Lake Nakuru National Park. It is similar to the smaller Crowned Hornbill (*not shown*) but the back colour is a greyer-brown often with pale feather edges, a combination that gives the bird a fairly scruffy-looking appearance. In flight, it glides more and flaps less than most other hornbills and shows plenty of white in the tail.

Male

Female

Female

Male

Nesting females are imprisoned in tree-holes where they perform 100% of the incubation duties. Like all wonderful mothers, they are great multi-taskers and use this period to moult their wing and tail feathers simultaneously – a great use of their time yet most unusual in the bird world.

☐ Eastern Yellow-billed Hornbill ◀
50 cm | 20"
A spot-winged hornbill of the dry north with a huge, banana-like bill. This is one of the more difficult hornbills to find in the Baringo area but possibly the easiest to identify. It is far less likely to be encountered in the lodge gardens than the red-billed species there and you may therefore need to search the hinterland nearby to increase your chances of locating one. This hornbill enjoys a wonderful symbiotic relationship with the Dwarf Mongoose: the cumbersome bird enjoys the benefits of locusts flushed by the mammal and the short-sighted mammal benefits from the extra vigilance provided by the birds.

☐ African Grey Hornbill ▲
50 cm | 20"
A medium-sized hornbill with a white eyebrow and scaly brown plumage. This bird prefers to feed in a variety of trees where it eats mostly fruits and invertebrates. It travels between trees and bushes with an undulating flight, looking rather like a flying walking stick on account of its slim lines and decurved bill. Birds stay in contact with loud, long, piped calls: *"kwi-kwi-kwi-KWEEo- KWEE-o"*.

159

◀ ☐ **Red-and-yellow Barbet**
22 cm | 8¾"
A brightly coloured barbet often associating with tall termite mounds in open savanna. There is no mistaking this charismatic bird of dry areas, and family groups are a joy to watch. The white spots in the plumage are much larger and more conspicuous than those of the duller D'Arnaud's Barbet which, unlike the Red-and-yellow Barbet, does not have red in the face or a red bill. They feed on a mixed diet of seeds and invertebrates and both nest and roost in termite mounds, a dominant pair often having sibling or offspring helpers. Pairs proclaim their territory with a ritualised duet that translates to a rambling "*red'n'yellow, red'n'yellow…*".

◀ ☐ **Red-fronted Barbet**
17 cm | 6½"
A common but inconspicuous barbet of lightly wooded bush. This medium-sized barbet is easily identified if the white throat and distinctive face pattern are seen. The red front to the crown is not always easy to see and is a feature that is shared with the much smaller Red-fronted Tinkerbird (*page 163*). However, the tinkerbird lacks the thick black line through the face. It nests in tree holes and is a frequent victim of the honeyguides (*pages 164–165*), which are brood parasites.

☐ **D'Arnaud's Barbet** 19 cm | 7½" ▼

A comical yellowish bird with black and white spots. It is common in dry bush and scrub, and is often seen sunning itself in the morning light. Barbets are close relatives of woodpeckers but this species tends to be more terrestrial in its habits. The longish tail is heavily barred, while the body is mostly yellowish with black spotting, giving the bird a rather scruffy appearance. Racial differences exist within the Rift Valley: birds north of Nakuru show a spotted cap while those south of Naivasha show a black cap. It is often seen in pairs, sometimes making cyclical, ratchety calls with their tails cocked proudly in the air.

Northern form
showing
spotted cap

Southern form
showing
black cap

☐ White-headed Barbet   19 cm | 7½" ▼

An unmistakable large barbet with a white head and tail. The bill of this bird is well-adapted to a diet of fruiting figs and other fruits although it will also feast on a variety of insects. It is common in the last-remaining fig forests in the southern Rift Valley and is relatively easy to find in the well-wooded gardens surrounding Lake Naivasha but becomes scarce further to the north. This barbet is sometimes seen in extended family groups and maintains contact with a series of grunts and growls. Confusion may be possible with the similar-sized White-headed Buffalo Weaver (*page 217*) but if identification is in doubt, check the colour of the rump and tail: these are white in the barbet, whereas the buffalo weaver has a red rump and dark-brown tail.

Spot-flanked Barbet
14cm | 5½"

A black-throated barbet of open bush and light woodland. This small barbet is usually heard before it is seen and calls a repeated series of "*kweerk*" notes that get faster with each note and sound quite excitable. It is very fond of fruits and with prolonged observation, you may see these birds regurgitate small waxy parcels of seeds onto branches or dropped on the ground. Ecologists believe that this bird, along with other fruit-eating barbets, returns a great service to its food plants by dispersing seeds.

Red-fronted Tinkerbird   10cm | 4"

A small and noisy barbet of dry bush and well-wooded areas. Although mostly black and white on the head, this finch-sized barbet shows much yellow on the wings and rump. As with the much larger Red-fronted Barbet (*page 160*), the red at the front of the crown is not always easy to see so you may want to look out for the heavily striped head and clean white throat instead.

Its monotonous "*ponk-ponk-ponk*" call may be repeated 20 or more times and is an easy call to remember. The similar Yellow-fronted Tinkerbird (*not shown*) is not found in the Rift Valley.

■ Greater Honeyguide

19 cm | 7½"

A vocal bird of light, open woodland. You are likely to hear these birds making their repeated, telephone-like, territorial call "*wheet-too*" well before you see them. The first view is usually of their distinctive black-and-white tail pattern as they fly off. The flash of white in the outer tail feathers is common to both honeyguides shown here – but be wary, as Klaas's Cuckoo (*page 144*) shows the same feature. Female Greater Honeyguides are basically grey below and dull brown above but males have a black throat and white cheeks. Immatures are similar to females, but have a blue eye-ring and a bright lemon-yellow wash to the throat and breast.

▶

Like cuckoos, honeyguides are brood-parasites, laying their eggs in other birds' nests for the host family to raise. However, honeyguides target different species, specializing in tree-hole nesters such as barbets and woodpeckers.

Male

Both sexes call a soft rattle which lures people and Honey Badgers to bee colonies, where both parties get to enjoy the spoils.

Immature

◼ **Lesser Honeyguide** 14 cm | 5½"

A shy sparrow-like bird with a dark, stubby bill and grey and olive-green plumage. This is a common resident of wooded areas but can be difficult to find since it often sits still for long periods. Unlike the Greater Honeyguide, it does not attract people or Honey Badgers to bee colonies, but still has a sweet tooth – enjoying beeswax and insects in equal measure – and is happy to feast on the spoils after a bees' nest has been raided by others. The call is a repeated number of "*chip*" notes.

◼ **African Grey Woodpecker** ▶
19 cm | 7½"

A common grey woodpecker of open woodland. This medium-sized woodpecker is the only one in the region to show a grey head and plain olive-green back. Males have a bright-red cap and both sexes show a red belly and rump, the latter being very conspicuous in flight. This bird is easy to find in woodlands that are dominated by the Yellow-barked Acacia and it often feeds on the ground, raiding ant colonies. Its call, a descending series of "*kwik*" notes, has a laughing quality.

Male

165

Like parrots and cuckoos, woodpeckers are zygodactyl, meaning that they have two toes directed forwards and two pointing backwards. Most other birds have one backward and three forward-pointing toes.

Female

Nubian
Woodpecker

Male

Nubian Woodpecker
20 cm | 8"
A large, spotted woodpecker of open bush and acacia scrub. A common visitor to old fallen trees, this woodpecker shows bold, dark spots on the underparts, pale spots on the upperparts with some fine, pale barring on the wings, and yellow shafts to the tail feathers. Males can be distinguished by their red cap and red 'moustache' (known as the malar stripe), whereas females show a black forehead peppered with white and no 'moustache'. Their flight is heavily undulating. Listen out for the loud call "*keek-keek-kee-kee*", which gets progressively slower and sounds like a bicycle hurtling downhill while applying bad brakes.

Cardinal Woodpecker 14 cm | 5¼"
A small, streaked woodpecker of woods and gardens, especially those of camps and lodges. A great place to start looking for it is where a collection of animal skulls is exhibited, for they routinely feed on the insect larvae that bury inside the horn of Wildebeest, Eland and Buffalo, to name a few. Unlike the other woodpeckers shown here, the underparts are streaked rather than spotted, and the back and wings show pale barring. The name Cardinal derives from the male's red cap, although female birds lack this feature.

Bearded Woodpecker 23 cm | 9" ▼

A large woodpecker with a black-and-white striped face. Although widespread in areas with plenty of mature trees, this grand woodpecker is nowhere common. Unlike the other woodpeckers in Kenya's Rift Valley, this bird shows dark underparts consisting of fine olive-green bars. The striped facial pattern is very obvious in both sexes. Males are identified by the bright red patch at the rear of the crown but otherwise the sexes are similar.

Male

Female

Female

Cardinal Woodpecker

Male

■ Rufous Chatterer
19 cm | 7½"
A small babbler with a yellow bill and rusty-orange underparts. Like other babblers, these birds hop around in family gangs but the contact call is a high-pitched squeaky whistle rather than raucous cackles. It is most common around the Lake Baringo area.

■ Arrow-marked Babbler
22 cm | 8¾"
A medium-sized, dark-brown bird of bushy areas. This gregarious species lives in extended family groups and its noisy scowls leading into raucous disarray are usually the first sign of its presence. The many small, white chevrons down the throat and chest account for its name. Adult birds show bright-yellow eyes, while those of immatures are darker. Birds sift through leaf-litter, tossing it like a salad, looking for small invertebrates before flying a short distance on stiff wings to the next stop.

■ Brown Babbler ▶
22 cm | 8¾"
A pale-faced babbler with bright golden eyes. This babbler is found north of the equator and its distribution does not overlap with that of the similar Arrow-marked Babbler, which is only found south of the equator. It shows similar white feather tips on the breast but these are not pointed as in Arrow-marked Babbler. It is easy to find in the camp gardens around Lake Baringo.

Black-lored Babbler 22 cm | 8¾"
A pale grey-headed babbler with white eyes. Very similar to Arrow-marked Babbler, this species is common in the central Rift Valley. It can be separated from that species by its frosty-grey forehead that contrasts heavily with the black lores (*i.e.* the area between the eye and the bill) and the white, rather than yellow, iris. The call has a laughing quality, "*wah wha-ha*".

169

◻ **Common Bulbul** 18 cm | 7"

An abundant brown bird with a yellow vent. This is the most widespread of all East African birds and there are few places where it is not found. You are most likely to see it in the grounds of camps and lodges where it becomes very familiar and invades food halls and buffets with regularity. The common call is a down-slurred "*he-wee-we-wer*", often accompanied with open, quivering wings.

As with many other members of its family, scrub-robins are highly territorial and not only sing a great deal but will also engage in fighting with rivals, sometimes to the death!

◻ **White-browed Scrub Robin**
15 cm | 6"

A widespread songbird of dry scrub with a broad, rufous tail and white in the wing. This spritely bird can look boring, brown and stripy one minute then brilliant the next – the difference all being down to the extraordinary rusty-coloured tail that can be fanned wide open with dramatic effect. There is quite a variation within this species throughout the Rift Valley: northern birds show a large white patch in the wing and grey in the head, while southern birds show two obvious wing bars and darker brown stripes on the breast.

Southern form

Northern form

Getting to know this
bird should be a
priority, as it is the
benchmark for reference
when describing the size of
many other songbirds.

■ Spotted Morning Thrush 17 cm | 6½" ▲

A heavily spotted rufous chat of dry and green thickets. Common in the Lake Baringo
and Lake Magadi areas, this rusty-brown songster is absent from the higher altitude
areas of the central Rift Valley. It is often quite approachable and may even feed from
the hand in the gardens of camps around Baringo. It sings a beautiful whistled song
throughout the day in between bouts of feeding, when it often drops from a low perch
to collect morsels from the ground. To the horror of many birders in East Africa, this
species has officially been renamed as Spotted Palm Thrush. However, since it is not
fond of palms, most people prefer to call it by its more familiar name.

☐ Common Rock Thrush 20 cm | 8"

A variable migratory chat of open areas. Males in their bright breeding plumage are only likely to be seen in the Rift in March and April, before they migrate north out of the region, and show a bright white rump. Most birds that are seen in the region, from October onwards, are much duller in colouration and usually appear heavily spotted. It spends a lot of time standing upright, in dry scrub on stony ground, and the tail appears quite short. This species is similar in size and proportions to Superb Starling (*page 204*) and is much larger than the resident Little Rock Thrush, which is wheatear-sized (*pages 120–123*).

▼

Despite their name and similarity in appearance, rock thrushes are members of the chat family and not related to the true thrushes, such as Olive Thrush on *page 174* .

Male

Male breeding
(March)

Male non-breeding
(November)

172

Little Rock Thrush 15 cm | 6"

A colourful, wheatear-sized chat. Both sexes show an orange belly and the head and breast are blue-grey in males and grey-brown in females. This feature helps to separate it from the male Common Rock Thrush in breeding plumage, which shows an orange breast and belly. These birds are most active very early in the morning and late in the evening but tend to be fairly inactive throughout the rest of the day. Look out for these birds close to rocky outcrops, especially around Baboon Cliffs and Makalia Falls within Lake Nakuru National Park.

Mocking Cliff Chat 21 cm | 8½"

Colourful thrush-sized chats of rocky cliffs and gorges. Males are very dark on the head, breast and back but show a brilliant white flash in the upperwing, whilst females are smoky-grey on the head, breast and back and lack the white wing patch. The bright-orange belly of males can be hard to see at times and the belly of females tends to be dark maroon rather than orange – a useful identification feature in comparison with the similar, but much smaller, Little Rock Thrush. It sings a sweet warble from steep cliff-faces mostly in the morning and late afternoon, several males sometimes singing in close proximity.

▼

Male

Female

☐ **Olive Thrush** 22 cm | 8¾" ▲
A common garden bird with a bright-orange
bill and dull-orange flanks, this otherwise
dull-brown bird is often seen probing for
worms on garden lawns in the region and
fills the same ecological niche as many other
thrushes around the world, such as the
American Robin and European Blackbird.
It likes to rest and hide away under bushes,
well away from the eyes of dangerous avian
predators, such as Gabar Goshawk (*page 106*).
Young birds are heavily spotted on the breast
and flanks. If you happen to be birding around
Lakes Naivasha or Nakuru, also keep your
eyes open for the African Thrush (*not shown*),
a western species that seems to be spreading
east. It is very similar in appearance and habits
to Olive Thrush but is greyer and has a
yellow bill.

☐ **Cape Robin Chat** 17 cm | 6½"
A common bird of gardens and
undergrowth with an orange
throat. This bird is fairly similar
to the larger and much brighter
White-browed Robin Chat but
identification should actually be
fairly straightforward: Cape Robin
Chat shows a grey belly and flanks,
brown rather than blue-grey
wings, and a brown rather than
orange at the back of the neck.
Both species are superb mimics of
other birds but this bird tends to
break for more pauses and is less
ear-piercing than the other.
It, too, is a frequent victim to
the Red-chested Cuckoo, the
notorious brood parasite.

☐ White-browed Robin Chat 20 cm | 8" ▼

With its striking head-pattern, grey back, bright orange underparts and burnt-orange tail in flight, this thrush-sized bird is easy to recognise. Common in lodge and camp gardens where there are large and scattered trees and lush undergrowth, the White-browed Robin Chat is naturally a shy bird though it can be easily tamed. The cyclical song starts quietly but increases in volume and tempo. Pairs will often engage in powerful duets, especially when rival pairs are nearby, and the noise can be deafening. It is common to see this bird feeding its young, which are heavily spotted and lack the strong face pattern of the adults. If you are very lucky you may also see adults feeding a dark, heavily barred fledgling that is far larger than itself – this will be a juvenile Red-chested Cuckoo (*page 143*), a species that routinely lays its eggs in robin chat nests.

■ Brown-crowned Tchagra 19 cm | 7½" ▲

A secretive, streaky-headed bird of bush and rank grass. Pronounced "chag-ra", this small, attractive bushshrike is common in suitable habitat in the southern Rift but is largely replaced by Three-streaked Tchagra in the Bogoria-Baringo area. As an indicator of habitat suitability, if there are Rattling Cisticolas (*page 192*) present you stand a good chance of finding this tchagra. The rich-chestnut wings help to separate the Brown-crowned Tchagra from similar bushshrikes, such as Black-backed Puffback (*page 185*). Its call is a sweet, reverberating, descending whistle "*TIU-TIU-tiu-tiu-tiu*". The closely related, and larger, Black-crowned Tchagra (*not shown*) can also be found in the Rift but its head pattern is more striking, with a whiter face and jet-black crown.

Brubru 14 cm | 5½"

A peculiar-looking bushshrike with a distinctive voice. This bird of dry scrub could be confused with a variety of other similar-looking species including the two tchagra species shown here but the Brubru has more white in the face and breast. The crown, back and wings are blackish in males and brown in females and both show off-white lines through the face, neck and wings. Also look out for the bright-chestnut flanks. The song is a distinctive, far-carrying rolling trill, "*prrrrrrrp-prrrrrrrrp*", not dissimilar to an old telephone ringing.

Three-streaked Tchagra 17 cm | 6½"

A small, plain-looking bushshrike of the dry north. Unlike the Brown-crowned and Black-crowned Tchagras (*the latter not shown*), this species does not show a bright stripe over the eye but does have three narrow black stripes, or streaks, on the grey head: one through each eye and one running from the bill over the crown. The cold grey-brown back contrasts markedly with the rich-chestnut wings, as in the other tchagra species. If you are fortunate to get a really close view of this bird, look out for a ring of silvery dots around the iris, a feature that may be unique among African birds.

▼

General note: Helmetshrikes are very sociable and noisy birds, always encountered in flocks in the mid-level and canopy of open woodland. Their camouflaged nests are built close to a tree trunk and pairs are often assisted by family members. Their excitable calls are loud and rather difficult to transcribe but often involve bill-snapping.

☐ **Grey-crested Helmetshrike** 25 cm | 10"

A rare bird with grey and white headgear. This helmetshrike is larger than the White Helmetshrike but never shows the yellow eye-wattles of that species and has a diagnostic upright, dark-grey crest. This special bird is endemic to East Africa and is threatened by two very different factors: habitat loss caused by humans, and loss of genetic integrity due to cross-breeding with the White Helmetshrike. Many odd hybrids between the two occur, especially around Nakuru and Naivasha.

▶

White Helmetshrike
20 cm | 8"
A gregarious pied bird with curly, white headgear. This species is very similar to the Grey-crested Helmetshrike but always has a bright-yellow ring of skin around the eye. Some birds show a white patch in the wing when perched, others appear mostly black, but all have a small white flash in the outer wing in flight and white tips to the tail. This species is widespread across sub-Saharan Africa and the various subspecies differ in the shape of the crest.

▼ ☐ Northern White-crowned Shrike
21 cm | 8¼"
A gregarious bird of dry scrub and low bush. Usually encountered in extended family groups, this distinctive shrike is dark-backed and pale-fronted. The pattern of white crown, dark line through the eye and black cheeks is unique among shrikes in the region and the bird shows an obvious white rump in flight. Young birds lack the white crown and are grubbier-looking. Social groups are noisy, giving a mix of nasal and chattering notes, including a Punch and Judy-like "*weer-haha*". For a long time, this species was placed in the same family as the helmetshrikes but is now considered to be more closely related to the true shrikes (*pages 180–181*).

Adult

Immature

179

Red-backed Shrike 18 cm | 7"

A migrant shrike of open bush with a black-and-white tail. Males have a blue-grey crown, neck and rump, a black face and rich-chestnut back. Females and immatures are brown on the head and back and show lots of scaly markings on the flanks. Good numbers arrive from Europe and Asia in October–November and then again on their return journey north in March–April, with only a few staying locally between December–February. The population has declined markedly in its breeding grounds in northern Europe, partly due to habitat loss and climatic changes.

▶

Grey-backed Fiscal
25 cm | 10"

A distinctive long-tailed shrike of open woodland and acacia scrub. The masked appearance of this bird, with grey crown, neck and back, are the best features for separating it from the Common Fiscal. Groups are sociable and engage in fits of tail-wagging while emitting squabbling calls from an exposed perch or sometimes from the ground. In flight, they appear very long-tailed and show a white flash in the wing and outer tail feathers.

Female

Male

The family of true shrikes, which includes the three species shown here, are commonly known as 'butcherbirds' on account of their habit of impaling their prey, mostly invertebrates, on thorns and maintaining a 'larder' for harsher times. These are not to be confused with the true butcherbirds that are found in Australia.

☐ Common Fiscal 23 cm | 9" ▼

A common pied shrike of open bush – the most abundant and widespread of the shrikes in southern Rift. Common Fiscals are blackish above and white below with an obvious white bar across the upperwing when perched and in flight. The sexes look similar although females have a small chestnut patch on the flanks. It is frequently encountered perched in the open during game-drives that pass through bushy areas. Young birds are browner and heavily barred. The soft song is a sad melody of "*twee*" notes.

This species is sometimes confused with the male Village Weaver (*page 219*) which is also yellow with a black head so check if you are unsure of your identification.

◻ **Black-headed Oriole** 21 cm | 8¼" ▲

A bright-yellow bird of open woodlands. As the name indicates, this bird shows a completely black head, although its bill is bright red. The back can show a hint of green and the central tail feathers are also rich olive-green. The flight feathers are mostly black but edged in white with a small white patch at the base. As with so many woodland birds, getting to know their calls is a great help when trying to locate them – so listen out for the oriole's strong, fluty "*weeeooo*" or descending "*weeo-weeoo*". Two other species of oriole can sometimes be seen in the Rift – Eurasian Golden Oriole and African Golden Oriole (*neither shown*) – but Black-headed is by far the most frequently encountered and the only one with a black head.

◻ **Grey-headed Bushshrike** 25 cm | 10"

A stunning bird of wooded areas that hops and glides through the tree canopy in search of a variety of prey, including small reptiles, large insects and, sometimes, young birds. Despite its bright plumage, it can be difficult to locate – so it is well worth familiarizing yourself with its unmistakable call, a drawn-out, mournful whistle "*pheeeeuuuu*", although it can also be heard making a variety of clicking calls and eerie, rising whistles. Generally secretive, every now and again one will put on a great show for you and be seen gliding on spread olive-green wings from one tree or bush to another. If you are this lucky, try to observe how other birds react to it – most will avoid contact with this glamorous but stealthy predator.

☐ Sulphur-breasted Bushshrike
17 cm | 6½"

A shy but brightly coloured resident of open woodland and acacia scrub. This bird is considerably smaller than the heavyweight Grey-headed Bushshrike and has a much slimmer bill. A good view will reveal the yellow forecrown that extends over the eyes. As with most bushshrikes, it is usually heard before being seen and it sings a sweet, whistled "*phew-pu-pu-pu-ruuuuuu*".

▶

Cuckooshrike, boubou and puffback

Male

Female

Black Cuckooshrike 20 cm | 8"

A long-tailed cuckoo-shaped bird of thick and open woodland. Males are glossy blue-black all-over and have an orange flange of skin at the base of the bill. Some birds show bright-yellow shoulder-patches. Females have pale and heavily barred underparts and olive-green on the back, with bright-yellow bars in the wing. They spend much of their time feeding on invertebrates gleaned from leaves in the tree canopy and the loud insect-like trill is usually heard before they are seen. Their movements are poorly understood although local birds are supplemented by migrants from elsewhere in Africa.

Tropical Boubou 21 cm | 8¼"

An easy-to-find bushshrike of open woodland and gardens. At first glance, this species appears all-white below and black above, including the eye, with a white bar running across the wing – but often reveals a peachy flush to the underparts. Given close views, the underparts will be seen to have a peachy flush.

There is a chance of confusion with the male Black-backed Puffback, which shares the same habitat – but the puffback is smaller and has a red eye. As with most bushshrikes, one feature of their behaviour is synchronized calling, known as an antiphonal system. This involves one bird starting the duet with a series of notes and the other bird coming in seamlessly to finish the harmony. Until you see this for yourself, you may find it hard to believe that it is not a single bird making the call, but in fact two. In the case of the Tropical Boubou, "*poo-poo*" by the male is followed immediately by "*wey-hoo*" from the female. You are just as likely to encounter the antiphonal phenomenon with Slate-coloured Boubou (*page 187*).

■ **Black-backed Puffback** 17 cm | 6¾"
A heavily marked, black-and-white
bushshrike of wooded gardens and open
scrub. It is fairly similar in plumage to the
smaller Chin-spot Batis (*page 198*), but
has a plain throat and underparts.
Males show a greater contrast between a
white belly and black back, while
the greyer females show a pale spot
between the eyes and the bill.
Both sexes have a red eye.
Their name derives from the male's
impressive display in which he puffs
up his white rump feathers into a fluffy
ball and calls loudly "*took-took-took*",
sometimes flying around with his back
still puffed-up. Males also emit various
whipped "*tikweeoo*" notes.

Female

Male

▶

The Tropical Boubou is fond of
other birds' eggs and nestlings
and is frequently seen being
harassed or chased by smaller
birds within its territory.

☐ **Common Drongo** 25 cm | 10"

A black, fork-tailed bird usually seen
perched high in a tree or bush. Often
referred to as the Fork-tailed Drongo on
account of the deep 'V'-shaped notch in
the tail, adult birds have completely glossy
blue-black plumage and a red eye. Immature
birds are browner with black flecks in the
plumage. They appear more thickset than
the slimmer Northern Black Flycatcher,
especially around the neck, and show
a thicker, slightly hook-tipped bill.
The rambling call is a mix of
squawks and peeps. ▶

Drongos are insect hunters and
often sit in exposed positions
waiting for their quarry to fly by
before swooping onto their prey,
revealing lighter matt-brown
flight feathers that contrast with
the black body and tail.

Juvenile

Adult

The Slate-coloured Boubou is a vocally versatile bird and, like the Tropical Boubou (*page 184*), has an antiphonal duet calling system. One call starts with a loud "*ch'shh-ch'shh*" followed by a woodblock-sounding "*coco-pop*". Another series starts "*pa-ponk-pa-ponk*" followed by "*wee-eer*" and you might also hear several loud "*queerk-queerk*" notes returned with a low "*donk*".

☐ Slate-coloured Boubou 20 cm | 8"

A noisy, dark sooty-grey bird of low vegetation in bush and open woodland. This bird can appear all-black but a good view reveals a softer grey plumage, especially on the back. Unlike the Common Drongo and Northern Black Flycatcher, it spends much of its time hopping on the ground or along low-lying branches and has longer, sturdier legs. It rarely perches high in a tree so this should be a consideration when separating it from the other species shown here. A really useful identification feature is that the top of the bill obviously cuts upwards into the feathers of the forehead. In the other species shown here, the forehead feathers circle the top of the bill without interruption.

▲ ☐ Northern Black Flycatcher
18 cm | 7"

A slim, black bird that perches in the middle of trees and bushes. Frequently overlooked by birders and guides, this common matt-black flycatcher lives up to its name when swooping from its perch onto small flying invertebrates. Unlike the Common Drongo, it rarely sits out in the open, preferring to sit midway up a tree or bush with some cover, and is rarely seen on the ground. Young birds (*right*) are heavily spotted with light-brown dots. It lacks the forked tail and pale flight feathers of the drongo and has dark rather than red eyes. The song is a soft, sweet refrain of quiet whistles and chips but it will sometimes mimic other species.

White-eyed Slaty Flycatcher ▲

15 cm | 6"

A blue-grey flycatcher with prominent white spectacles. This species is common in a variety of woodland and gardens, particularly those with a number of Yellow-barked Acacia trees. It tends to be less active than other flycatchers, usually sitting quietly on an exposed perch waiting for prey to fly by and swooping to catch it in mid-air, but sometimes feeds by dropping to the ground. This bird appears a soft blue-grey all-over with a slightly paler belly and obvious white eye-rings. Like the young of the Northern Black Flycatcher (*page 187*), the young of this species are heavily spotted with pale feathers but show the outline of an emerging white eye-ring. Its call is an agitated "*chrrrr-chrrrr*".

African Paradise Flycatcher

breeding male 36 cm | 14"; female 17·5 cm | 7"

A stunning chestnut and sooty-grey bird, sometimes with a very long tail. Despite its serene appearance, this is an aggressive, territorial bird that will often chase birds far larger than itself. They catch insects in swooping flights, often hovering before resting on a perch to eat. Males in breeding plumage show an impressive long tail that can be at least three times the length of the head and body combined. Outside the breeding season, the tail streamers are lost and the males then look similar to female and immature birds. The amount of white in the plumage depends on the local gene pool: some populations show none at all yet, at the other extreme, some male birds, such as the male from Lake Baringo opposite, have entirely black and white plumage that is devoid of any chestnut colouration. The sharp contact call "*schwee-shurp*" sounds like the snapping of garden shears.

Male

Male
white
form

Female

An intricate nest
of moss, feathers
and spiders' web
are fused together
between two
branches, often
near human
habitation where
the birds feel safe.

☐ **Spotted Flycatcher** 14 cm | 5½"

A migrant brown flycatcher with a streaked breast. Only likely to be encountered in the Rift between October and April, this visitor from Europe and western Asia is the easiest of the three brown flycatchers to identify due to the obvious streaking on the crown and breast. It catches insects on the wing, taking off from an exposed perch and swooping onto its prey before returning to the same or a nearby perch. It prefers open woodland (like Pale Flycatcher) to dry acacia scrub (as does African Grey Flycatcher) but newly arrived birds could turn up anywhere.

▼

African Grey Flycatcher

14 cm | 5½"

A small, grey bird with a lightly streaked crown. It has a rather large head for its body size and the black eye in the plain face gives it a rather 'beady-eyed' appearance. Often found sitting upright on the outer branches of an acacia or other small bush in the dry belt, this rather plain flycatcher is usually found in small, loose family parties. Rather than taking flies on the wing, as with the African Paradise Flycatcher (*page 188*), this bird generally drops to the ground for its quarry. You are more likely to hear its "*shree-shree*" alarm call than its simple song.

▼

Pale Flycatcher 17 cm | 6½"

A plain-looking flycatcher of open woodland. This resident flycatcher is similar to both other flycatchers shown here but is slightly larger, and has a plain head without any streaking on the crown. It also appears more slender in shape, perhaps due to its longer tail, and is a warmer grey-brown in tone.

Another useful identification feature is that the flight feathers do not show bold white edges, which are a noticeable feature in African Grey Flycatcher.

▼

Rattling Cisticola 14 cm | 5½"

The classic 'little brown job' (LBJ) of bush and scrub. This abundant small, brown warbler is heavily streaked above and pale below, with a relatively thick bill. It shows a brown crown that is lightly streaked but this is more chestnut in tone in immature birds. The tail is broad and rudder-like, edged with white spots that are evident in flight. Among the noisiest of small birds, it can often be heard shouting many harsh rasping notes that are followed by the rapid rattle "*chr-chr-chr-chr*". Compare this species with three other cisticolas on *pages 130–131*.

▼

Grey Wren Warbler 13 cm | 5"

A dark sooty-grey warbler of the dry country. This dull warbler, a close relative of the Grey-backed Camaroptera (*page 194*), can frequently be heard in the open scrub north of Nakuru and south of Naivasha. Its distinctive "*chuk....chuk....chuk*" call, that sounds like two pebbles being struck together, once every second, is quite unforgettable. Identification of non-calling birds is very straightforward as it is the only all-dark warbler of open scrub. It frequently raises and fans its white-tipped tail but is otherwise fairly obscure.

Tawny-flanked Prinia
11 cm | 4¼"

A tiny brown bird with a long tail. Although appearing rather dull at first glance, the Tawny-flanked Prinia has a lot of personality for its size. It is often found in small, active groups that engage in frantic bouts of tail-swinging and calling – a zipping "*cheerp-cheerp*". Birds can be quite tame at times and a close approach will enable you to see the red eye and white eyebrow. The warm-brown flanks help to separate it from some other 'little brown jobs' (LBJs). Around Lake Baringo, this bird is replaced by the similar Pale Prinia (*not shown*), which shows a whitish belly and lacks tawny flanks.

☐ **Yellow-breasted Apalis** 13 cm | 5" ▲

A long-tailed, green warbler with a white throat and belly and a bright-lemon breast. The head shows variable amounts of blue-grey and the back is moss-green. A busy little bird of open bush and leafy scrub, the Yellow-breasted Apalis is often found in pairs or family groups. Within Kenya's Rift Valley, two distinct forms of this species occur: birds of the dry north show less grey on the head, a brown tail and a plain yellow breast, while birds of the southern and central Rift show more blue-grey on the head, a green tail and, in males, a black spot on the yellow breast. Their songs are fairly similar: green-tailed males start with "*territ-territ-territ*" (like a galloping horse) to which the female responds with a rising "*kerker-keer-keer-keer*". Brown-tailed males sound faster and females respond by growling.

☐ **Grey-backed Camaroptera**
10 cm | 4"

A tiny grey-and-green warbler with a short tail. You stand a good chance of seeing this bird wherever there are trees with a rich understorey of vegetation, where it can be quite approachable. The grey head and back are complemented with moss-green wings. One feature you may observe when birds are hopping through the lower branches of dense vegetation is how white the feathers are under the tail. Birders will sometimes jest that it is called the 'camera-operator' because its call is similar to a camera with a whirring motor-drive shooting many frames "*di-der-der-der-der-der*".

Grey-capped Warbler 15 cm | 6" ▼

A vocal, green-backed warbler with a grey crown.
This widespread but shy bird is frequently encountered
wherever there is dark, damp and tangled vegetation,
often near lakes and small streams. It will sing loudly
from the undergrowth – *"wuhu-chit-chit-chit-chit"*
– but you may have to be patient for a bird to reveal
itself. The grey crown contrasts with a narrow,
black face-mask and, with a very good view,
you may see a small, rusty-coloured bib.

■ Northern Crombec 7·5 cm | 3" ▲

A distinctive short-tailed bird of dry
open scrub. The white throat and brow
over the eye are usually quite obvious
and the underparts show a strong wash
of cinnamon-buff. Often found in pairs,
these attractive little balls of feather
are fairly common in lightly wooded
bush north of Nakuru and in the Lake
Magadi area, where they are usually
seen dangling from the end of branches.
The tail is very short and rarely visible,
a feature common to all crombecs, and
the legs are surprisingly long.

■ Red-fronted Warbler 11 cm | 4½"

A tiny brown warbler with clean
white underparts and a very long tail.
Another LBJ (little brown job) of the
dry northern and southern ends of Rift,
this little fellow is very active when
singing, raising his tail and "buzzing"
noisily. Otherwise it is fairly obscure
and feeds low down in open scrub. Both
sexes show a rich rufous cap and the tail
is black, tipped with white, which looks
impressive when males are tail-wagging.

■ Buff-bellied Warbler 10 cm | 4" ▼

An active, small and plain-looking warbler. This charming little bird is very common where acacias persist. It lives in family parties and is always on the go, moving from one tree or bush to the next and rarely staying still. It is greyish-brown on the upperparts, including the crown, and much paler below. Despite its name, this warbler is usually more buff-coloured on the face than on the belly, which often appears white. Birds call frequently to stay in contact with each other, a trilled "*chit-chit-chit...*".

Male

Female

Chin-spot Batis 10 cm | 4 ▲

A small black, white and grey bird of open woodland and scrub. Both sexes show a grey crown and back, yellow eyes and a broad, white line through the wing. Males have a thick black band across the chest, while females show a distinctive rusty-brown spot on the chin (hence the name) and a thinner breast-band of the same colour. If you see one bird of a pair, then the other will be nearby. These attractive birds have a distinctive "*pee....poo*" call, the latter note being much lower than the first, which is often accompanied by snappy and burry notes. Despite their flycatcher-like behaviour, the batises are more closely related to shrikes.

African Yellow White-eye
11 cm | 4½"

A small yellow bird with a bright, white eye-ring. Common in a variety of leafy habitats, including gardens, throughout the Rift, this songbird is usually encountered in small flocks gleaning their food from the ends of branches. They are bright yellow below and olive-green on the back and tail. The similar but smaller Abyssinian White-eye (*not shown*) is lime-yellow on the back and shows a narrower white ring around the eyes – but is only likely to be found south of Lake Naivasha.

White-bellied Tit 13·5 cm | 5½"

A small, black-and-white bird of open woodlands and well-wooded gardens. These birds generally feed from the mid-canopy and higher in a variety of trees, making the white belly easy to observe from below. A view of the upperparts is not always easy but does reveal a white shoulder-patch and white edges to the wing feathers. Birds are vocal and are frequently located by their scolding calls, "*see-cha-cha*".

☐ **Rüppell's Starling** 35 cm | 14"

A long-tailed, glossy starling with white eyes. Similar in general appearance to the Greater Blue-eared Starling (*page 203*), the Rüppell's Long-tailed Starling, as it used to be known, shows a long, graduated tail that befits the old name. Its obvious white eyes contrast with the matt-black head. The colouration of the body plumage varies among birds of different age and sex. Most show a deep-purple gloss with a green sheen to the wings, but some birds appear an iridescent cobalt-blue. They are highly vocal birds that sing a continuous, noisy chatter and whining, sometimes in the middle of the night; in flight their wings produce a whooshing sound.

▶

See Rüppell's Vulture (*page 90*) to discover more about Wilheim Rüppell.

These gaudy blue starlings are typically vocal but if you notice them becoming particularly noisy and agitated, it might be worth investigating further as they frequently harass predators, such as owls and birds of prey. Do proceed with caution, however, as they also mob dangerous snakes!

☐ **Red-billed Oxpecker** 22 cm | 8¾"

A red-billed 'tick-bird' found on mammals. Oxpeckers can be found on a variety of mammal species from which they famously collect ticks and other skin parasites. However, this apparently symbiotic relationship is not always what it seems. For as well as feasting on a variety of parasites and, strangely, ear-wax, oxpeckers are very happy to open wounds and drink the blood of the host, especially Hippos that are frequently scarred and wounded in territorial fights. The Yellow-billed Oxpecker (*not shown*) was formerly abundant in the Rift Valley but has almost disappeared along with many of the larger mammal species on which it used to feed. It is suspected that Red-billed Oxpeckers continue to prevail locally because they are more accepting of domestic livestock. Although bill colour is the obvious feature used to separate the two species, Red-billed Oxpeckers also have a yellow eye-ring and a uniform brown back, rump and tail; Yellow-billed Oxpeckers show a pale rump.

Wattled Starling 20 cm | 8"

A mostly plain-grey starling. Males sport impressive black and yellow headgear during the breeding season but females and non-breeding birds are fairly drab looking. They breed in good numbers in the Rift Valley and then gather in vast flocks that typically head onto the higher grasslands of the Masai Mara and Serengeti to follow the wildebeest migration. Although often seen riding the backs of various mammals, they prefer to feed on the invertebrates disturbed by the game rather than directly off the game itself (unlike the oxpeckers). In flight, they are easily identified by their white rumps that contrast with their black flight and tail feathers.

Breeding

Non-breeding

Elephants are the only large mammals that will not tolerate oxpeckers on their skin, as it is very sensitive to the sharp claws of these birds.

☐ **Bristle-crowned Starling** 42 cm | 17"

A chestnut-winged starling of cliffs and gorges in the north. Superficially similar to the more common Red-winged Starling, this bird is substantially larger in the body and shows a much longer tail that tapers and becomes very slim towards the tip. It shows similar orange-chestnut wing patches in the open wing but these can be difficult to observe on birds that may be sitting high on the cliffs. The 'bristle-crown' is in fact a pad of velvety feathers that rises above the bill towards the top of the head. This feature is present on both sexes but is slightly smaller on the otherwise identical female. This is another of the 'Baringo Specials' that make the journey north so worthwhile, but may also be encountered in the Samburu and Shaba National Reserves to the east.

▶

Immature

Adult

Red-winged Starling

◀ ☐ Red-winged Starling 30 cm | 12"

A chestnut-winged starling of towns, villages and rocky areas. This bird is mostly glossy-blue-black with a long, pointed tail. The 'red' in the outer flight feathers of the wing, after which the species is named, is actually orange-chestnut. The sexes are fairly similar but females show a dark smoky-grey head that merges with some dark streaking on the breast. Although still found inhabiting the rocky hillsides of the Rift, flocks have also made themselves quite at home on the tall buildings in Nakuru and other conurbations, and are easily located by their oriole-like "*tu-wee-oo*" whistle.

▲ ☐ Greater Blue-eared Starling
23 cm | 9"

A large, glossy starling with orange-yellow eyes. It is both common and widespread in the wooded areas of the Rift Valley and may also be encountered on the plains. It can be quite bullish in the company of other birds. This green-glossed starling shows a violet-blue sheen around the ears and belly in good light. The song is a jumbled mix of chittering warbles, but the call is easy to remember if you can imagine an old woman with a whining voice calling her husband Pat in for supper – "*pa-a-at*".

▼ □ Superb Starling 19 cm | 7½"

A common and widespread, multicoloured bird of open bush and plains.
Often encountered in family groups, the Superb Starling lives up to its name with its
'coat of many colours'. When separating adults from the similar Hildebrandt's Starling,
look for the obvious white line that divides the blue breast from the orange underparts,
and the white eyes in its black face. In flight it shows white under the wing and often
calls a cheerful "*cheera-cherr-eet*".

Young Superb Starling
can be separated from
Hildebrandt's of the same
age by their dark breast
and white vent.

Adult

Immature

Adult

Female

Male

☐ Hildebrandt's Starling 19 cm | 7½"

A colourful, red-eyed starling of dry, open scrub. Very similar in appearance to the more common Superb Starling, Hildebrandt's Starling is only likely to be encountered in the dry sector of the Rift Valley south of Lake Naivasha. It can be distinguished from Superb Starling by its red, rather than white, eyes and lack of a clean white line between the blue breast and orangey belly. The belly also tends to be more light-peach in colour than the bright orange of Superb Starling. In addition, its back tends to appear much darker blue and this colour extends to the shoulder; in Superb Starling the shoulders are green. In flight, it shows the same peach colour of the belly in the underwing, rather than white. The song comprises a series of slow-paced "*woo-wah*" notes mixed with chattering.

See Hildebrandt's Francolin (*page 133*) to discover more about Johann Maria Hildebrandt.

▲ ☐ Violet-backed Starling
17 cm | 6¾"

A small starling of open bush and woodland. Unlike the other starlings in this book, the sexes of this species are very different. Males show white underparts and a brilliant, iridescent, violet-coloured back, which accounts for its other names – Amethyst or Plum-coloured Starling. Females are light-brown above and pale below but show dark streaking throughout. Flocks of these birds typically move into the Rift from the south during March, with some birds staying year-round to breed. In poor light, be careful as the glossy male can appear to be just black-and-white. It sings a series of quickly trilled notes.

Male

Female

■ **Variable Sunbird** ▶

11 cm | 4½"

A small sunbird of gardens, open
woodland and dry scrub. Females
are dull grey-brown above and
yellowish-green below, but the
variety of colours in the male is
a sight to behold! These are very
busy birds that barely keep still –
which does not particularly help
when you are trying to identify
them! To separate the male
from the similar but
smaller Collared
Sunbird, look for a
blue or purple wash
across the face and
breast. You may also see
a small orange feather or
two between the wings and
the breast – the pectoral tufts.
The song is a series of rapid and
rising "*chit-chit-chit-chit*" notes.

Female

Male

Eastern Violet-backed Sunbird
12cm | 5"

A white-bellied sunbird of dry, open country with a short bill. Males are among the most attractive of all dry-country species with their vibrant purple head and back, which contrast elegantly with the snow-white underparts. A good view may also reveal a shining turquoise-green shoulder-patch. Females are typically less colourful and show a simple two-tone colouration: brown head and back contrasting with white underparts, but also look out for the white stripe over the eye. Both sexes may show rusty staining on the face caused by pollen from their food-plants. They are fond of a variety of flowering plants in the bush but also look out for them on aloes in the gardens of camps and lodges in the dry north.

Collared Sunbird 10cm | 4"

A tiny, green-and-yellow sunbird. More restricted to mature woodland than the other sunbirds in this book, the Collared Sunbird is often seen feeding in trees rather than bushes and its diet includes more invertebrates. The sexes are quite similar – green above and lemon below – but males show an iridescent green breast underlined with a narrow, purple border. The song is less harsh that the other sunbirds – a sweet, piercing "*see-yu*" repeated many times. The tiny nest of this bird is frequently raided by the brood-parasite Klaas's Cuckoo (*page 144*).

▼

Female

Male

Scarlet-chested Sunbird

Female

Male

Marico Sunbird 12·5 cm | 5"

A small, dark and fast-moving sunbird of open woodland. Males show a glossy-green head, back and upperwing, and a black belly. Given a good view in good light, the breast shows a conspicuous broad maroon band running across it that is buffered with light blue above. Females are typically nondescript with an olive-brown back contrasting only slightly with the buffy-olive underparts that are neatly spotted on the breast and belly but not the throat. Immature males are very similar to females but show a blackish throat. Where present, these sunbirds will attend multi-species flocks that gang-mob owls and other predators with repeated aggressive calls.

◄ Scarlet-chested Sunbird
15 cm | 6"

A large, dark sunbird, with a long, decurved bill, that inhabits woodland edge and gardens. Males are all black with a spectacular red bib that is flecked with silvery-blue. In good light, they also show a green forehead, throat and moustache. Females are dark chocolate-brown, especially on the head, and have light streaking towards the vent. Immature males appear similar to females but are paler and show a hint of the red bib. The song is a rapid series of "*chip*" notes. Look out for these birds feeding on aloe plants in gardens.

Male

Female

Amethyst Sunbird 14cm | 5½" ▼

A robust-looking, dark sunbird of gardens and woodland edge.
Males often appear black from a distance but better views in
good light will reveal an iridescent green cap and ruby throat
that does not extend down the breast, (unlike Scarlet-chested
Sunbird). A small, ruby-coloured shoulder-patch may also
be seen. Females can be difficult to separate from the
other female sunbirds shown
here but they have a pale
throat, heavier streaking
on the flanks and a
clear white stripe
over the eye.

Female

Male

▢ Beautiful Sunbird

breeding male 15 cm | 6"; female 8 cm | 3½"
A brilliantly coloured sunbird with a long
tail, found in gardens and thorny scrub.
Quite unlike the other long-tailed sunbirds
shown here, breeding males are mostly
iridescent green with a bright orange-
red breast-band bordered with yellow
patches on the flanks. The tail is black, and
reasonably short, save for the two long,
treamer-like, central tail feathers. Females
are rather plain with a grey-brown head
and back and very pale underparts, usually
cream-coloured, but can be yellowish.
Immature males are similar to females but
have black throats. Non-breeding males are
grey-backed, and most have long central
tail streamers and a green patch on the
shoulder. Both sexes are comparable in size
to the Variable Sunbird (*page 206*).

▢ Tacazze Sunbird

breeding male 23 cm | 9"; female 15 cm | 6"
A large, dark and long-tailed sunbird
with a strong purple wash. This beautiful
sunbird of the highlands migrates to
lower elevations during the cool winter
months (between May and September).
It is easily overlooked on account of
its similarity to the more common
and widespread Bronze Sunbird but
its shows a brilliant purple hue to its
shoulders, back and chest. Females are
similar to female Bronze Sunbirds but
are greyer and lack the yellow wash to
the underparts. Flowery gardens in the
Naivasha area are perhaps the best place
to search for this special bird.

The name of this bird comes from the
Tacazze River in northern Ethiopia, close to
where the first specimen was collected.

Male

Female

Non-breeding male

Male

Female

Tacazze Sunbird

Male

Bronze Sunbird

Female

Non-breeding male

◻ Bronze Sunbird ▲
breeding male 22 cm | 8¾"; female 12·5 cm | 5"

A large, dark and long-tail sunbird with a strong bronze-wash, found in gardens and tangled scrub. This common sunbird is both noisy and conspicuous and among the easiest to identify. Males appear dark but shine coppery-bronze in good sunlight, often with a greenish hue on the head (although this is not always visible). The underparts and tail are blackish and the central tail feathers very long. Females show a strong yellow wash to their underparts, a clean white throat and stripe over the eye that contrast with the darker feathers on the cheeks. Their shorter tail is dark brown, like the back, but shows white outer feathers. This sunbird sings a rambling chitter but you are more likely to hear the more frequent piercing "*chu*" call notes.

☐ House Sparrow 14 cm | 5½"

A common species that will probably be familiar to visitors from most parts of the world. The House Sparrow was introduced to the coast of East Africa around 100 years ago but has now spread across southern Kenya, from one village to the next. Males show a distinctive head-pattern: white cheeks; a large, black throat-patch bleeding into the top of the breast; a grey crown; and dark-chestnut at the back of the neck. Females are very bland, lacking much in the way of colour. Both sexes have dark eyes, unlike the Kenya Rufous Sparrow, adults of which have white eyes. House Sparrows give a classic, monotonous chirping call.

The House Sparrow is one of the most successful bird species in the world and occurs on all continents apart from Antarctica. Although it is an introduced species in East Africa, it is quite passive and does not appear to pose a threat to other native species.

☐ Kenya Rufous Sparrow 14 cm | 5½"

The native equivalent of the House Sparrow that is common throughout the Rift. Both sexes can easily be told from House Sparrow by their white eyes, and males have grey rather than white cheeks. Although females lack the 'sparkle' of the males, they are still more colourful than female House Sparrows and often show chestnut on the back and warm tones to the face.

Male

Female

Male

Female

■ Grey-headed Sparrow 17 cm | 6½" ▼

A widespread sparrow of bush and gardens. This local race of the variable Grey-headed Sparrow 'super-species' is known as Parrot-billed Sparrow, on account of its large bill, and may well be a species in its own right. Like the other sparrows shown here, it is very much at home in the company of people, feeding primarily on the ground. Its calls are quite unmusical, mostly dry "*chips*" and not much else. It possesses a white bar in the wing although this is not always easy to see.

The nest of the Grey-capped Social Weaver is an untidy bundle of dry grasses, often on the outermost branches of a Whistling Thorn acacia, and sometimes shows a prominent entrance hole. Occasionally, pairs will combine nests making a double- or even treble-sized nest that is shared.

☐ Grey-capped Social Weaver 11 cm | 4½" ▼

A very small, brown weaver likely to found in large colonies in the acacia-rich dry lands. A busy colony may exceed 100 birds and you are likely to find them by hearing their busy calls, a series of "*chew-chew-chew*" notes. Obvious identification features include the creamy-grey cap and the very short tail that has a whitish tip.

◀ ☐ Speckle-fronted Weaver
11 cm | 4½"

A small, sparrow-like weaver that is common in barren areas of acacia scrub in the southern sector of the Rift. It is best identified by the chestnut-brown patch at the back of the neck, but also look for the speckled forehead, although this can often be difficult to see. It has a pale face and appears rather beady-eyed, setting it apart from other small birds in the same flock. The nest tends to be more hidden than those of most other weavers, often being situated low down in an acacia rather than hanging from the end of a branch

▼ ☐ Yellow-spotted Petronia
15 cm | 6"

A plain-looking sparrow with a pale bill, found in open scrub and dry woodland. This species is so plain and boring that it makes a Grey-headed Sparrow look exciting – but maybe that is part of its charm? It has a be-spectacled appearance and pale edges to the flight feathers. The yellow spot on the throat after which it is named can be difficult to see and is frequently absent. It is a humble and non-aggressive species and its presence is often only noted when its dry "chirrup" call pierces the air. It feeds on the ground, picking up seeds, but flies a short distance into a tree to survey the scene when disturbed.

The Yellow-spotted Petronia is a resourceful species as exemplified when the author witnessed a pair nesting in the brain-cavity of a dead Giraffe's skull that was hung for decoration in a camp. Keeping its feather-lined nest so close to people, and away from danger, enabled it to raise at least one healthy brood!

215

☐ White-billed Buffalo Weaver 22 cm | 8¾"

A very large and dark weaver of the dry north. Males
are essentially black all-over but often show a scruffy
white shoulder-patch and an ivory-coloured bill that
shows an obvious bulge at the base and turns dark
in non-breeding birds. Females are dark brown and
heavily striped below but never show a pale bill.
They feed on the ground and are easiest to find
at Baringo and Bogoria, the latter being the
southernmost part of their extensive breeding
range that extends westwards to Senegal.
The nest is huge, sometimes exceeding
one metre in length, and is built
mostly from thorny twigs and
almost no grass.

▶

☐ White-browed Sparrow Weaver   17 cm | 6¾" ▲

A common brown-and-white striped weaver of dry open country and acacias.
Usually encountered in family groups, this gregarious bird is very approachable and will
frequently feed at your feet. It shows a conspicuous white eyebrow, two white bars in the
wing and a white rump that is obvious in its lazy flight. The sexes are similar. This species
builds a very untidy nest of brown grass (not green grass like the 'yellow' weavers) in
busy colonies. Oddly, the nest has a single entrance hole until the point when the eggs
hatch, at which time a second hole is created. It is most common north of Nakuru and
in the southern sector of the Kenyan Rift close to Lake Magadi.

◀☐ White-headed Buffalo Weaver   18 cm | 7"

An unmistakable large weaver with a white head and underparts, dark back and bright
red rump. This bird is easy to find in the dry bush of the north as it often gathers in open
trees and shrubs along roadsides. It is a colonial breeder but the nests are well dispersed
across a wide area so there may only be one or two nests per tree. The nest itself is very
large in relation to the size of the bird, and is typically more twiggy than the grassy nests
of other weavers such as the White-browed Sparrow Weaver. This may be what appeals
to the Pygmy Falcon (*page 107*) which, in East Africa, prefers to use a vacated White-
headed Buffalo Weaver nest to that of any other species. Look out for the white wing
patches when the bird is in flight and listen out for the loud, parrot-like "*cheeya*" calls.

217

The nest of Village Weaver hangs from a long 'stalk' and has an obvious bulbous chamber.

The nest of Speke's Weaver is an untidy ball of grasses with an entrance hole facing downwards, sometimes with a short tunnel.

The nest of Lesser Masked Weaver is usually built in acacia over water and is spherical with an obvious but not very long entrance tunnel.

Male

Female

Village Weaver

Speke's Weaver

Male

Female

Male

Female

▲ ☐ **Lesser Masked Weaver** 13 cm | 5"

A small, masked, yellow weaver with cream-coloured eyes and blue-grey legs. This weaver is widespread in the Rift Valley but may go unnoticed in the presence of the bolder and more vocal Village Weaver. Males show a black mask which, like Village Weaver but unlike Speke's Weaver, covers half the crown – and the very pale eyes are really noticeable. The back is poorly marked and generally appears greenish. The female is more similar to Speke's Weaver than to Village Weaver on account of the pale eye, but her bill, legs and feet are always blue-grey in colour.

☐ **Village Weaver** 17 cm | 6¾"

A large, stout-billed, gregarious weaver with a red eye. Large colonies can often be found in acacia trees overhanging water. Breeding males are best identified by their black face that extends above the forehead, and the heavy black stripes running down the back (compare also with Vitelline Masked Weaver, *page 225*). Females and non-breeding males lack the black face and heavy streaking on the back, instead showing greyish backs and a yellow throat and breast, and a yellow or white belly. The call comprises a series of dry "*chip*" notes, while the song is a heady mix of wheezing and electronic-sounding "*whee*" notes.

☐ **Speke's Weaver** 15 cm | 6"

A common, masked, yellow weaver with a yellow eye. This species is quite similar to the widespread Village Weaver but can easily be separated by the following features: an all-yellow crown above the black face-mask that encloses the bright-yellow eye, its more slender bill, and an evenly spotted back without black stripes. Females are dull grey-brown, show just a faint lemon-wash across the breast and a pink base to the bill that often appears even more slender than the males. This is a gregarious species that nests in large colonies and is most common south of Nakuru.

Female

Male

The nest of Little Weaver is tiny and fits easily into the palm of an adult's hand. It is spherical with an additional entrance tube and is so finely woven that it sometimes appears transparent in places.

The nest of Golden-backed Weaver shows an obvious dome-shape, lacks an entrance tunnel and is always situated over water.

▲ ■ Little Weaver 10 cm | 4"

A tiny, masked weaver of dry open woodland and scrub. Due to its small size, this diminutive weaver could be mistaken for an odd warbler or sunbird. The yellow in the male's plumage is more lemon-yellow than golden-yellow, as with most other weavers, and the eye is dark – but otherwise the main identification feature is its very small size. The plain-looking females appear especially warbler-like but have the stout bill typical of the weaver family. It is less gregarious than some other weavers but joins mixed flocks at bird tables.

■ Golden-backed Weaver 13 cm | 5"

A distinctive weaver with a black hood and neck and dark-chestnut underparts. A bright blaze of yellow on the back runs all the way down the rump. The eye is bright-red but can be difficult to see against the black hood. Non-breeding males appear very tatty but often show the tell-tale signs of black against an otherwise yellowish head. Females are very similar to female Northern Masked Weaver but show a heavily streaked back and a warm buffy wash to the yellowish underparts. This weaver is rarely found far from water and has a patchy distribution with small populations being found elsewhere in western and southern Kenya.

The nest of the Northern Masked Weaver is similar to that of Golden-backed Weaver but is less domed and more spherical.

☐ **Northern Masked Weaver** 13cm | 5"

A black-and-brown-masked weaver with dark-brown eyes. The dark face-mask of male birds is unique in the Kenyan Rift because it gradually merges from a black core to a rusty-brown colour around the entire edge. The dark eyes of both sexes serve to separate it from Lesser Masked Weaver (*page 219*). Females are also similar to female Golden-backed Weaver but are typically less yellow underneath and show a stouter all-black bill. In Kenya, this species is only found around Lake Baringo and is much sought-after. It is always found close to water, often associated with other weavers.

▼

Female

Male

Often called Jackson's Golden-backed Weaver. See Jackson's Widowbird (*page 128*) for more about Sir Frederick Jackson.

Male

Female

The nest of the Spectacled Weaver (*below*) is very distinctive, having a long, tube-like entrance hanging from the side of the main chamber.

The nest of Holub's Golden Weaver (*not shown*) is similar to that of Black-necked Weaver but the entrance tube is much shorter and rarely extends lower than the main chamber of the nest.

▼ ☐ Spectacled Weaver 14 cm | 5½"

This unobtrusive yellow weaver with a moss-green back and wings is aptly named on account of its black eye-mask that accentuates the yellow eyes, giving it a 'spectacled' appearance. Both sexes usually show a warm-orange glow to the face and males also have a black throat. Often found in gardens and well-wooded areas. The call is often the first sign of its presence – a rapid, high-pitched, downward run of "*pipipipi*" notes. The similar Baglafecht Weaver (*page 224*) has a black back and black wings with yellow markings.

Male

Female

☐ Holub's Golden Weaver 18 cm | 7" ▼

A large, bright-yellow weaver of gardens and woodland edge, with a stout black bill. It has pale-yellow eyes and a lime-green back. The sexes are similar; females have some green on the crown and neck; males have an orange throat, but this can be hard to see. It is not a colonial breeder and is usually seen alone or in pairs. The call is a loud "*chup*" repeated once every few seconds.

Male

Female

Female

Male

The nest of the Black-necked Weaver shows a long entrance tube but not as long as that of its close relative the Spectacled Weaver.

▲ ☐ **Black-necked Weaver** 14cm | 5½"
A black-backed, yellow-fronted weaver of dry scrub. This smart-looking bird is a close relative of the Spectacled Weaver and has a similar narrow, pointed black bill. Both sexes have a black back, wings, tail and eye-mask, but can be told apart as males have a black throat and yellow crown and females have a yellow throat, black crown and yellow eyebrow. In Kenya's Rift Valley this weaver is only likely to be encountered in the south, close to Lake Magadi, where it is not uncommon. The similar Baglafecht Weaver (*page 224*) differs in having yellow edges to the wing and tail feathers.

The nest of the Grosbeak Weaver is an elegant and tightly woven dome of fine fibres, usually built among tall reeds, that shows an obvious folded-back entrance hole at the side.

Female

Taxonomists have determined that this weaver has no close relatives and may in fact not even be a weaver at all!

Male

☐ **Grosbeak Weaver** 17 cm | 6¾" ▲

A very large and chunky-billed dark-brown weaver of swamps and reedy margins. Identification is fairly straightforward as males are solid-looking birds with a white forehead and white flashes in the wing. Females are lighter brown and show extensive streaking on the underparts and a yellow base to the bill. They are highly gregarious and form substantial flocks in wetland areas. It is often called the Thick-billed Weaver.

☐ **Baglafecht Weaver** 15 cm | 6"

A pale-eyed weaver with black neck and cheeks. This distinctive bird is often found in pairs or small family groups. Males have black cheeks, neck and back, with fine yellow lines down the wings and tail. The similar females show an all-black crown and face. The bill is black, slender and pointed and the call is a buzzing, down-slurred trill.

Male

◀ ■ **Vitelline Masked Weaver** 13 cm | 5"
A common weaver throughout the Rift. Similar to
the larger Village Weaver (*page 219*), but easy to tell
apart given a good view. Both species have red eyes
and a warm-chestnut border to their black face-
mask, but the black on a male Vitelline Weaver's
face does not extend onto the crown or
breast, and the back lacks any strong
black streaking. Female Vitelline Weavers
generally have a warm-buff breast and
flanks that contrast with the white belly, and
a pale, narrow bill; female Village Weavers
have a yellow breast and a dark, heavy bill.

The nest of the Vitelline Masked Weaver (*left*) is
very easy to identify as it is always onion-shaped
and rarely shows an entrance tube.

Female

The Baglafecht Weaver does not
nest in colonies and the untidy nest
(*right*) is often attached directly to
a main branch rather than dangling
down like a Village Weaver's nest.

Male

Female

225

☐ Common Waxbill 10 cm | 4"

A common red-masked 'finch' of grassland and open bush, often close to water.
Usually encountered in flocks dangling from grassy seed-heads, these dainty little
birds show a bright-red waxy-looking bill, red 'bandit's mask' and white on the chin.
Otherwise they are mostly brown, though a close-up view will reveal fine barring to
the plumage and a black belly. If you see one you are likely to see many.

▼

Waxbills are very popular cage birds and many have escaped from captivity in various parts of the world. Common Waxbills now live wild in Brazil, Spain and Portugal and on many islands in the Atlantic, Pacific and Indian Oceans.

☐ Crimson-rumped Waxbill
10cm | 4"

A pale-looking finch with splashes of red in the face, wings and rump. This attractive little bird is similar in size and appearance to the widespread Common Waxbill but shows far less barring in the plumage and a generally black bill with a small amount of red at the base (rather than all-red as in Common Waxbill). It feeds on grasses and shows an even greater attraction to areas close to water than Common Waxbill. The sexes are similar but immature birds lack the red face-mask.

▲ ☐ Black-cheeked Waxbill
10cm | 4"

A dry-country finch with a black face and red rump. Most of the plumage is pinkish-grey and the wings are heavily barred. It is a scarce species and only likely to be encountered in the dry north near Lakes Baringo and Bogoria. It is also rarely approachable and distant views are all you may be able to obtain of this attractive bird. The very similar Black-faced Waxbill (*not shown*) occurs in the very south of the region, near Lake Magadi, and shows black on the belly and under the tail. Rather confusingly, in southern Africa that species is also known as Black-cheeked Waxbill.

Male

Female

◀ ▢ Pin-tailed Whydah
breeding male 30 cm | 12"; female 10 cm | 4"

Small, seed-eating birds with a variety of plumages. Breeding males display impressive long tail-streamers which they dangle in a hanging flight over the drab brown females while calling continuously "*tsweet-tsweet-tsweet*". Non-breeding males look similar to the stripe-headed females but retain a red bill and have more white in the face. They are closely related to the Village Indigobird (*page 232*) and, like that species, are a brood-parasite of the waxbill family, especially those on *pages 226–227*. However, unlike cuckoos and many other brood-parasites, whydahs and indigobirds do not evict the eggs of the host family and their chicks grow up with the rest of the brood.

▢ Red-cheeked Cordon-bleu
13 cm | 5"

A delicate waxbill with bright-blue underparts and light-brown back. Frequent in open bush, gardens and lightly wooded areas, you may also see them in villages, often in pairs, mixing with the Red-billed Firefinch (*page 233*). The common call, a high-pitched "peet-pit-pit-pit", is quite similar to that of the firefinch. The sexes look similar, both having pinkish bills and brown crowns, but females lack the dark-red cheekpatch of the male. They are a common host to the Pin-tailed Whydah, a brood-parasite of the waxbill family

◀ ☐ **Blue-capped Cordon-bleu**
13 cm | 5"

A pink-billed blue waxbill of dry country. This species looks very similar to the Red-cheeked Cordon-bleu but males are easy to identify on account of their all-blue head that lacks the red cheeks and brown crown of that species. Unaccompanied females are more difficult to separate from female Red-cheeked Cordon-bleus but typically show more blue in the face and more brown below – and always a pale-pink bill. In both sexes the tail is longer than that of the Red-cheeked Cordon-bleu. This species is restricted to dry habitats, notably around Lake Baringo in the north and Lake Magadi in the south.

Male

Female

Female

Male

This small finch is also known as the Melba Finch in southern Africa.

Female

Male

◀ ☐ Green-winged Pytilia
14 cm | 5½"

A brightly coloured finch of dry scrub. Males show a bright-red face and a yellow breast-band but otherwise the sexes are quite similar, both having a grey head, green back and wings, red rump and tail, heavily barred grey flanks and a red bill. They are sometimes seen in association with the Eastern Paradise Whydah, which is a brood parasite that lays its eggs in pytilia's nests. Because of their preference for thorny bushes, getting a good look at these birds is not always easy – but it is worth making an extra effort to follow them around as eventually they may relax and afford wonderful views.

▼ ☐ Bronze Mannikin
9 cm | 3½"

A tiny, brown waxbill with a white belly. Often occurring in small numbers in well-wooded areas and gardens, these birds also gather in flocks to feed on grass seeds at the woodland edge. The mostly dark-brown plumage shows barring on the flanks and in good light the shoulders show a dark green gloss. The bill is short and stout, typical of granivorous (seed-eating) birds. It is most frequently heard in flight, when the short, buzzing "*pee-pu*" call catches the attention.

■ Eastern Paradise Whydah" ▼

breeding male 38 cm | 15"; female 13 cm | 5"

An unmistakable bird of arid areas, male Eastern Paradise Whydahs in breeding plumage are among the most beautiful of all African birds, sporting enormous black tails that may exceed three times the bird's own length. They display to prospective females with short bouncing flights around their territory when they appear quite ridiculous. In sharp contrast, females and non-breeding males are very dull brown but show dark stripes running over the head. As brood-parasites, their distribution is directly linked to that of their host, the Green-winged Pytilia, which is most common in the northern Baringo–Bogoria area and also in the dry south, near Lake Magadi.

Male

Female

Male

Female

☐ **Purple Grenadier** 13 cm | 5" ▲

A stunning purple-and-brown waxbill.
Widespread in dry bush and scrub,
although rarely seen in numbers, this
beautiful little bird shows a brown back,
violet-blue rump and dark tail in both sexes.
Males have patchy purple-blue areas on the
breast and belly, while females show brown
bars below. Both sexes have decorative
colouration around the eyes – dark-blue in
males but light-blue and studded in females.
It is often found feeding near the base of
bushes and thickets, giving a soft, high-
pitched call "*tseet-tseet*" as it moves around
– a sound you may struggle to hear.

☐ **Village Indigobird** 10 cm | 4" ▶

A tiny black bird with a white bill
and pink legs. Usually found in
close association with the Red-billed
Firefinch, male indigobirds are easy
to pick out in the crowd. Females are
slightly more difficult to identify due to
their drab brown plumage but can be
separated from the very similar female
Pin-tailed Whydah (*page 228*) by their
plain breast that lacks any stripes.

◀ ☐ **Red-billed Firefinch**
10 cm | 4"

A tiny red-and-brown waxbill. These little 'finches' are common ground-feeders that associate with sparrows and doves in villages, towns and gardens, often in small flocks. Males are deep-red, like a fine claret, with a red-and- grey bill. The back is brown and you may be able to see many tiny white dots on the breast and flanks. Females are light brown all-over, have a distinctive red rump, and typically show brighter white spots on the underparts than males. This firefinch frequently associates with the Village Indigobird, which is a brood-parasite dependent upon this species. The similar African Firefinch (*not shown*) is less frequently encountered but birds of both sexes show a black vent and a silver-blue bill.

Male

Female

Male

Female

Village Indigobirds are part of the whydah family, which are brood-parasites, and specialize in laying their eggs in the nests of Red-billed Firefinch. Strangely, the host does not seem to mind sharing its home with the indigobird and the young grow up with a healthy bond.

233

☐ White-bellied Canary 11 cm | 4½"

A yellow, lightly streaked canary with a white belly. This species prefers dry scrub and feeds quietly on the ground, flying only a short distance when disturbed. In addition to the white belly, both sexes can be identified by the streaking on the flanks and mottled back, and females show some light streaking on the breast. It is a confiding bird that is quite at home in and around villages.

▼

Female

Male

African Citril 11 cm | 4½" ▲

A yellow-and-green canary of undergrowth and gardens. Looking quite similar to other closely related canaries (*opposite*), males show a black face that contrasts markedly with the bright-yellow underparts and stripe over the eye. Females are heavily streaked on the head and breast and both sexes show two yellowish wing bars. Small groups tend to be inconspicuous but may be found along hedges and in lightly-wooded areas throughout the region.

Brimstone Canary 14 cm | 5½"

A chunky canary of gardens and open areas with all-yellow underparts. Like most canaries, this species is mostly yellow with a moss-green back and crown but this bird has a heavy pink bill. The wings show two clear bars and there are bold yellow stripes over the eyes. Unlike the White-bellied Canary, it does not show a bold yellow rump in flight. It is easily attracted to bird-seed and feeders in gardens.

Male

◼ **Cinnamon-breasted Bunting** ▶

15 cm | 6"

A stripy-faced bird with brick-red underparts of rocky areas with scattered trees. Males show a black head with three white stripes on each side of the face, while females show a similar pattern with cream-coloured stripes on a dark brown head. It is thinly distributed along cliffs and escarpments, usually in pairs and rarely in small groups. The viewpoint at the top of Baboon Cliffs in Lake Nakuru National Park is a good place to find this species, which was formerly known as the Cinnamon-breasted Rock Bunting.

Golden-breasted Bunting 15 cm | 6"

An attractive bird with a golden-yellow breast and a striped head. These birds are widespread in the Rift where there is open woodland and dry scrub but are easiest to find around Lake Nakuru. They are shy and often take flight when disturbed from the ground (where they feed), but often just into a nearby tree or bush allowing close inspection. Given good views you will see a mix of black and white stripes on the head and two white bars in the wings. The mostly yellow breast has an orange hue that shines like gold in good light. They are most often encountered in pairs, never in flocks, and males sing their twittering song from an exposed perch high in a tree – a delightful "*tee-tu-tee-tu*" ending with a pronounced "*pee-chew*".

Streaky Seedeater 14 cm | 5½" ▼

A heavily streaked brown canary of bushy areas. The sexes are similar in this rather dull-looking species but the intricate array of stripes and streaks is attractive in its own right. The streaking extends from under the white throat all the way to the tail and it shows a heavily marked face. It appears more 'leggy' than other canaries and the buntings, which tend to be rather low-slung, and hops with its belly well off the ground.

■ **Barn Owl** 35 cm | 14" ▶

The white owl. This owl appears longer-legged than most others and has a heart-shaped face with jet-black eyes. At night, listen out for its loud, screaming "shriek" call. Like most other owls, this enigmatic species is secretive and shy but it often roosts in buildings in towns and villages, emerging at dusk to feed on rats and other rodents. It is among the most cosmopolitan of all birds and is found on all the continents apart from Antarctica.

Unlike most other owls, the Barn Owl's middle claw is pectinate (meaning that it has a serrated edge), an adaptation for preening. Other bird families with pectinate claws include nightjars and herons.

■ **Slender-tailed Nightjar** 25 cm | 10" ▼

An amazingly camouflaged nocturnal bird of open acacia areas. Difficult to find on the ground, nightjars are easier to see as they rise to hawk for insects at dusk and dawn, sometimes coming to feed on moths at the lights of lodges and camps, when they look like a falcon or a large swift. This is the most abundant of the five species of nightjar resident in the Rift and hence is the one you are most likely to encounter, especially around Lake Baringo where the resident bird guides know exactly where to find them. At night, listen out for its monotonous call which is similar to a car alarm "*we-we-we-we-we…*"; in flight, its call is a squeaky "*wik-wik-ik*".

Male

Female

As with all owl species, female African Wood Owls are larger than males.

■ African Wood Owl 35 cm | 14" ▲

A medium-sized brown owl of woods and gardens. This owl has a large, dark, round head with dark eyes set within a pale face. The breast is flecked with white and the underparts are heavily barred cream and brown. Unlike the larger eagle owls, this species does not have ear-tufts. The African Wood Owl may be heard duetting throughout the night – males beginning with a low and eerie "*woo-hoo woo-hoo*" followed by the female's higher-pitched reply "*oo-hoo-hoo-oo-hoo*". It feeds on a variety of rodents, birds and reptiles.

Grey form

Brown form

African Scops Owl

17 cm | 6¾"

A tiny and cryptically camouflaged grey or brown owl of woods and tangled gardens. This amazing little owl is almost invisible when roosting in trees by day and you may need an expert guide to show you one, particularly at Baringo where they are not uncommon. The best way to find one for yourself is to imitate the call very early in the morning and follow the reply. That call is a simple purred whistle "*prruu*", which is repeated every five seconds or so. The African Scops Owl feeds mostly on insects and amphibians.

Owls in East African lore

In many Western cultures, owls have long been associated with wisdom, wizardry and witchcraft but have not suffered a great deal for this perception. Across Africa, and especially in East Africa, owls are widely considered as symbols of imminent death to a family member and, consequently, many are killed on sight regardless of the truth that it is good luck to have them nearby. After all, they are the safest and most efficient form of pest control known to Man. For this reason, it is best not to share the whereabouts of owls unless you know that the people you are talking to are wise to this fact and not likely to harm them. Details of an injured owl orphanage are given in the Useful resources section on *page 245*.

◀ ■ Northern White-faced Scops Owl
25 cm | 10"

A very secretive small owl with a white face and orange-yellow eyes. This owl is among the most difficult to find and goes to great lengths to hide away when roosting in the daytime. It usually sits deep within thorny trees in arid areas and clenches its body feathers tight to its body that makes it appear 'sucked in', and the facial feathers are also contorted to give it a cat-like appearance. At night, the white facial disc is clearly outlined with a black border. The specialist bird guides at Baringo usually have a pair staked out and this may be your best chance of seeing one.

This small owl regularly takes insects, small birds and mice as part of its diet, but a bird was recorded taking a ground squirrel that was almost certainly larger than itself!

◀ ■ Pearl-spotted Owlet   19 cm | 7½"

A tiny, spotted owl of open scrub and wooded savannah. Despite its small size, not much bigger than a sparrow, this fearsome little predator regularly takes small birds and sometimes small mammals and reptiles as well as large invertebrates. It is primarily nocturnal but can also be active during the day. The large, bright-yellow eyes glare and you may also notice the neat pair of white eyebrows. On the back of the head is a pair of black 'false eyes' which may intimidate predators. The chest is streaked with chestnut-brown and the bird gets its name from the numerous small creamy spots on its back. The commonest call is a continuous piped "*peu-peu-peu*" that rises to a crescendo and finishes with long whistles. This is a useful call to learn, since many small birds are attracted by it and fly in to mob the dangerous owl.

All Eagle Owls across the world exhibit 'ear tufts' or 'horns'. They are not related to the ear structure at all but are just feather tufts with the technical name of plumicorns.

◀ ■ **Verreaux's Eagle Owl**
66cm | 26"

A huge owl of bush and open woodland. This is the largest owl in Africa and the third largest owl species in the world. It is very powerful and capable of killing prey such as small antelope, small cats and large snakes. They are highly territorial birds and adult males may fight to the death. However, they are more often seen perched in open trees at first light or at sunset, when their distinctive silhouette stands out clearly. In the middle of the day, they will generally roost out of sight in a large tree. The deep, booming "*hoo-hoooo*" call is not dissimilar to that of the Southern Ground Hornbill and sometimes these birds are attracted to the calling owls. Young birds often call a painful, drawn-out "*eee-errrr*" that is repeated over and over.

Named after the Frenchman J. P. Verreaux (1807–1873), a prolific bird specimen collector.

■ **Spotted Eagle Owl** 48cm | 19"

A large grey owl with yellow eyes, found south of the equator. As with the Greyish Eagle Owl, check for eye colour and which hemisphere you are in when identifying this bird. Spotted Eagle Owls often pick a territory with more established trees than Greyish Eagle Owls but are just at home on rocky cliffs. Their food is very varied and ranges in size from cockroaches to hares.

■ Greyish Eagle Owl ▶

45 cm | 18"

A large grey owl with dark eyes found north of the equator. Numerous technical features can be used to separate this bird from Spotted Eagle Owl but eye colour and geographical location are by far the easiest to use in the field. This owl is most likely to be encountered on rocky outcrops in semi-desert, especially at Baringo.

Greyish and Spotted Eagle Owls were formerly considered just one species but have recently been split into two on account of structural differences between their feet and legs, and overall size. The differences in plumage are subtle, subjective and not 100% reliable.

Birds are capable of crossing the equator and exceptions do occur so check those eyes if you can!

Useful resources

Suggested further reading

The Birds of East Africa: a Photographic Guide by Adam Scott Kennedy and Brian Finch. (in prep.). Publication expected in 2015 by Princeton **WILD**Guides.

The Birds of East Africa by Terry Stevenson and John Fanshawe. Published in 2002 by Christopher Helm.

eGuide to Birds of East Africa. An app version of Stevenson and Fanshawe's *Birds of East Africa* that contains the calls of over 1200 species. It can be downloaded at **www.mydigitalearth.com**.

The Birds of Kenya and Northern Tanzania by Dale A. Zimmerman, Donald A. Turner, David J. Pearson, Doug Pratt and Ian Willis. 2nd Edition published in 2005 by Christopher Helm.

I highly recommend these books to anyone interested in taking their birding to the next level, and for East African explorations beyond the Rift Valley.

Whose Bird? By Bo Beolens and Michael Watkins. Published in 2003 by Christopher Helm.

The anecdotes about the people that have birds named after them were gleaned from this book, which is a highly interesting read.

Birds of Africa: South of the Sahara by Ian Sinclair and Peter Ryan. 2nd Edition published in 2010 by C Struik.

The most comprehensive field guide to the birds of this incredible continent.

Checklist of the Birds of Kenya (4th Edition) Published in 2009 by the Bird Committee. Nature Kenya/East Africa Natural History Society

A very useful and affordable resource for anyone birding in Kenya.

Online resources

www.naturekenya.org
The very friendly and professional team is always there to assist in any matter relating to the wildlifeof Kenya and I highly recommend joining the organization.
www.surfbirds.com
A great website with up-to-date bird news from around the world. It is also a great place to showcase the bird images from your safari.

www.peregrinefund.org
A non-profit organisation that is dedicated to saving birds of prey from extinction. T
hey are among the most active in tackling the current crisis affecting East African vultures.

www.ted.com/talks/munir_virani_why_i_love_vultures.html
Forget your negative preconceptions about vultures and listen to someone who really understands them in this truly inspiring TED talk.

Useful contacts

For Bird Guiding at Lakes Baringo and Bogoria, call Francis Cherutich on (+254) 0723 163267 or email him at frankrutich@yahoo.co.uk.

To arrange visits to see the endangered Sharpe's Longclaw on the Kinangop Plateau with researchers that monitor them, call Jack Kiiru on (+254) 0726 562607 or (+254) 0735 840281, or email him at jackkiiru50@yahoo.com.

Should you find an injured owl or bird of prey in the region, please contact Sarah Higgins at the Naivasha Owl Centre on (+254) 0723 786007 or email her at kijabe@africaonline.co.ke. The website is **www.naivashaowls.org**.

Acknowledgements

Such a book would not be possible without the help of many people so I would like to take this opportunity to thank those who have assisted me along the way.

First and foremost, I would like to thank my wife Vicki for her support of my numerous bird projects and allowing me to use some of her wonderful images in this book but, most of all, I'd like to say thanks for being my wife and looking out for me.

During my numerous journeys to Lakes Baringo and Bogoria, one person has worked so hard to find me the birds I really wanted to see and photograph, my guide and friend Francis Cherutich. From my conversations with many top birders in Kenya and beyond, I know that I am not alone when I say that he is right up there with the very best local guides on the planet. Sadly, there are no awards or prizes for this type of skill but I hope that these few words will serve the same purpose of recognition for being the best. Thank you Francis.

For some great days out birding, informed discussion and tasty snacks (excluding marmalade toasties!), thanks to Brian Finch and Nigel Hunter.

For their generosity in providing accommodations, fabulous hosting, friendship and support I would also like to thank the following: Lulu Keeble and Graham Roy (Lime Catering, Kenya), Dudu Beaton (Bushfit & Kamakazi), Patrick and Karen Plumbe, Steve and Vicky Rose, Tony and Betty Archer, Nigel Archer (Nigel Archer Safaris) and Mike Cheffings (Bateleur Safaris).

Finally, to the team at **WILD**Guides: Rob Still, Andy and Gill Swash, and Steve Holmes and Brian Clews – designer, editors and proof-readers extraordinaire – thanks for making this book my favourite so far!

Photographic credits

All images included in this book were taken by the author, Adam Scott Kennedy, with the exception of the following:

Greg & Yvonne Dean (WorldWildlifeImages.com): Black-crowned Night-heron, adult (*page 34*); Common Ringed Plover, both images (*page 67*); Little Stint, both images (*page 70*); Giant Kingfisher (*page 78*); Banded Martin, perched (*page 89*); Gabar Goshawk (*page 106*); Eurasian Hobby, perched (*page 108*); Common Kestrel, male and female perched (*page 109*); Winding Cisticola (*page 130*); Blue-spotted Wood Dove (*page 139*); White-throated Bee-eater, perched (*page 150*); Eurasian Bee-eater, perched (*page 150*); Spot-flanked Barbet (*page 163*); Olive Thrush (*page 174*); African Grey Flycatcher (*page 191*); Buff-bellied Warbler (*page 197*); Marico Sunbird, male (*page 209*); Green-winged Pytilia, pair (*page 230*); Golden-breasted Bunting (*page 236*); Northern White-faced Scops Owl (*page 241*).

Steve Garvie (flickr.com/photos/rainbirder): Northern Red Bishop, breeding male perched and female (*page 129*); Eastern Yellow-billed Hornbill, both images (*page 158*).

Vicki Kennedy (rawnaturephoto.com): Blue-cheeked Bee-eaters (*page 11*); Lake Elementeita (*page 12*); Kinangop grassland (*page 18*); Lake Baringo (*page 21*); Three-banded Plover (*page 66*); Martial Eagle (*page 94*); Woodland Kingfisher (*page 149*); Rufous-crowned Roller (*page 154*); Eurasian Roller, perched (*page 155*); Three-streaked Tchagra (*page 177*); Pearl-spotted Owlet (*page 241*).

Paul Oliver: Golden-backed Weaver, female (*page 221*).

Andy & Gill Swash (WorldWildlifeImages.com): Little Egret, in flight (*page 32*); Cattle Egret, in flight (*page 32*); Glossy Ibis, in flight (*page 47*); Northern Shoveler, pair (*page 54*); Ruff, female and immature male (*page 60*); Blacksmith Plover (*page 72*); Gull-billed Tern, breeding plumage (*page 76*); White-winged Black Tern, breeding plumage in flight (*page 77*); Whiskered Tern, breeding plumage in flight (*page 77*); Yellow Wagtail, 'Blue-headed', 'Yellow-headed' and Sykes's (*page 80*); Alpine Swift (*page 82*); Barn Swallow, perched (*page 88*); Long-crested Eagle, in flight (*page 101*); Montagu's Harrier, female in flight (*page 102*); Pallid Harrier, female in flight (*page 102*); Bateleur (*page 105*); Eurasian Hobby, in flight (*page 109*); Rufous-naped Lark, both (*page 117*); Grassland Pipit (*page 118*); Capped Wheatear (*page 120*); Abyssinian Wheatear, pair (*page 121*); Northern Wheatear, pair (*page 122*); Pied Wheatear, pair (*page 123*); Diederik Cuckoo (*page 144*); Eurasian Bee-eater, in flight (*page 151*); Eurasian Roller, in flight (*page 155*); Hemprich's Hornbill (*page 158*); Red-and-yellow Barbet, (*page 160*); Red-backed Shrike, pair (*page 180*); Grey Wren Warbler (*page 193*); Red-billed Oxpecker (*page 201*); Beautiful Sunbird, female (*page 210*); Beautiful Sunbird, male (*page 210*); Crimson-rumped Waxbill (*page 226*); White-bellied Canary (*page 234*); African Citril, male (*page 235*); Cinnamon-breasted Bunting (*page 236*).

Roger Tidman: Montagu's Harrier, male in flight from above (*page 102*).

Maps

The maps on *pages 23–25* are adapted from maps licensed under the Creative Commons Attribution 3.0 Unported license (http://creativecommons.org/licenses/by/3.0/deed.en) Files used: Kenya_relief_location_map.jpg; Kenya–topographic_map-fr.svg.

Scientific names of the bird species included in this book

Most of the guides working in the Rift Valley use English names when referring to the birds they see. However, given the diversity of countries from which visitors to the region come, these names may not be familiar to all. Some visitors will, however, know birds by their universally accepted scientific name. The following list therefore includes all the birds mentioned in this book, ordered alphabetically by their scientific name. It is cross-referenced to the English name(s) used and the page number(s) on which the bird appears. English names are highlighted in **bold** for those species that are illustrated. For ease of reference, the page number for the main account for each species is shown in **bold**; other places in the book where a photograph appears are shown in *italics*. The other species mentioned in the book that are not illustrated are shown in normal text.

Index

Names in **bold** highlight the species that are afforded a full account.
Bold numbers indicate the page number of the main species account.
Bold blue numbers relate to other page(s) on which a photograph appears.
Normal black numbers are used to indicate the page(s) where the species is mentioned,
but not illustrated. For scientific names, see *pages 247–251*.

Ostrich female